COOKING OF

# SPAIN

D1324679

# COOKING OF SPAIN

Over 65 delicious and authentic regional Spanish recipes shown
step by step in more than 300 stunning photographs **PEPITA ARIS**

**southwater**

This edition is published by Southwater,
an imprint of Anness Publishing Ltd,
Blaby Road, Wigston, Leicestershire LE18 4SE;
info@anness.com

www.southwaterbooks.com; www.annesspublishing.com

If you like the images in this book and would like to investigate
using them for publishing, promotions or advertising,
please visit our website www.practicalpictures.com
for more information.

Publisher: Joanna Lorenz
Editors: Susannah Blake and Elizabeth Woodland
Copy-editor: Rosie Hankin
Photographer: Nicki Dowey
Home Economist: Lucy McKelvie
Assistant Home Economist: Emma McKintosh
Stylist: Helen Trent
Designer: Nigel Partridge
Production Controller: Wendy Lawson

© Anness Publishing Ltd 2013

NOTES
Bracketed terms are intended for American readers.
For all recipes, quantities are given in both metric
and imperial measures and, where appropriate,
in standard cups and spoons.
Follow one set of measures, but not a mixture,
because they are not interchangeable.
Standard spoon and cup measures are level.
1 tsp = 5ml, 1 tbsp = 15ml, 1 cup = 250ml/8fl oz.
Australian standard tablespoons are 20ml.
Australian readers should use 3 tsp in place of 1 tbsp
for measuring small quantities.
American pints are 16fl oz/2 cups. American readers should
use 20fl oz/2.5 cups in place of 1 pint when measuring liquids.
Electric oven temperatures in this book are for conventional
ovens. When using a fan oven, the temperature will probably
need to be reduced by about 10–20°C/20–40°F. Since
ovens vary, you should check with your manufacturer's
instruction book for guidance.

Medium (US large) eggs are used unless otherwise stated.

Main cover image shows Seafood Paella – for recipe, see page 45

PUBLISHER'S NOTE
Although the advice and information in this book are believed
to be accurate and true at the time of going to press, neither
the authors nor the publisher can accept any legal
responsibility or liability for any errors or omissions that
may have been made nor for any inaccuracies nor for any
loss, harm or injury that comes about from following
instructions or advice in this book.

# CONTENTS

# THE SPANISH CUISINE

The history and religion of Spain are visible on the plate. It is always true, to some extent, that what we eat says who we are. But in no country is it more obvious than in Spain. Ingredients, cooking methods and many recipes all have an easy-to-trace and fascinating past. And Spain's most famous foods – chorizo, cocido, gazpacho, bacalao, paella – have an encoded history.

## MOORISH INFLUENCES

"A land which hovers between Europe and Africa, between the hat and the turban" was Richard Ford's description of Spain in 1845. The Moors invaded Spain from North Africa, in AD711, and stayed for nearly 800 years. The Moorish influence is still evident today. To start with, a huge number of food words are derived from the Arabic: aceite (oil), arroz (rice), albóndigas (meatballs), almendras (almonds), almirez (the mortar) and almuerzo itself, the word for lunch.

In the mosques and palaces of Cordoba, irrigation systems were planned, making possible wonderful gardens such as the Generalife in Granada, as well as Valencia's rice fields. The valleys of the Guadalquiver

and Granada bloomed. The grey-green olive and the newly introduced almond transformed the landscape, while orange and lemon trees filled courtyards and surrounded buildings. New crops were planted, including sugar, spinach, aubergines (eggplant) and mint.

From the Moorish cuisine came new culinary methods – cooking in sealed clay pots and wood-burning ovens were introduced. The meat skewer and kebabs arrived, and churrasco (pieces of meat cooked on the barbecue) is still

*Above (left and right): Many classic desserts such as fritters drenched in honey and rich fruit syrups show the Moorish origins of much Spanish food.*

a Spanish favourite. Frying with olive oil and preserving in vinegar (escabeche) were both Arab practices, the latter eagerly adopted by the locals for preserving surplus fish for a little longer. The mortar and pestle could grind nuts to a smooth cream, used to thicken chilled soups such as the almond ajo blanco (white garlic soup) or salmorejo (a cream of garlic, bread and vinegar). Both were forerunners of the classic chilled soup, gazpacho.

Many things that are now considered typically Spanish come from this era: almond pastries, fritters in honey, milk puddings, quince paste, peaches in syrup, iced sorbets (sherbets), raisins and pine nuts used together in sauces, and the "caviar", botargo.

The spices brought by the Moors included cinnamon, cumin and nutmeg, served with chicken the way they are now, and the magnificent golden saffron. They enjoyed sour-and-sweet (agridulce) mixtures and anise bread. Look around in Spain now and you will find all these things still on the menu.

*Left: The Spanish love to cook and eat outdoors and cooking pieces of meat on skewers over a barbecue comes from the Moorish tradition.*

*Right: The slow-cooked stew of meats and chickpeas, cocido, was inspired by the Jewish sabbath stew, adafina.*

## CATHOLICISM CONQUERS

The *Reyes Católics* – the Catholic kings, Isabella and Ferdinand – conquered Granada, the last Moorish stronghold, in 1492. They threw out the Moors and the Jews, who were the Moorish managerial class, to make one united Catholic kingdom. The Jews, who had been in Spain for many centuries, left several imprints on Spanish cuisine, including cocido (meat and chickpea stew). The Christmas roscón has common features with the sticky braided challah, the Jewish Sabbath loaf.

The new foods enjoyed in this era were spectacularly different, favoured almost entirely for their religious orthodoxy. Bacalao (salt cod) was for Church fast days, of which there were some 200, when abstinence from meat – and sex – were required. Pork, which neither displaced peoples would touch, became an integral part of Spanish religion, and therefore everyday life. Eating sausages became a statement of loyalty and proof, if required, of conversion to the Catholic church.

*Below: Of all the spices that the Moors brought with them to Spain, rich golden saffron is the one most distinctively associated with Spanish cooking.*

### Cocido, the national dish

It is ironic that the cocido, that pot of long-cooked meats with chickpeas, is the legacy of a people whom the Spanish rejected. Its origins lie in the Jewish adafina, the Sabbath casserole, cooked the night before, and also served in three courses. Pelotas are

*Below: Since the days of the Catholic kings, pork sausages such as spicy red chorizo have become the main meat eaten in Spain.*

still added to cocido on big occasions. These are balls of minced (ground) meat or chicken livers, bread and pine nuts that echo the hamine eggs that the Jews added to adafina.

Adopted by the Catholic Spaniards, pork and sausages were added to the other meats in the cocido, as proof that the eaters were neither Jewish nor Muslim. Made almost entirely with meat, it was at first a thoroughly aristocratic dish. Then, as more chickpeas and potatoes were added, so it slipped down the social scale. Every region adds its own vegetables, and the further from Madrid, the more of a rural puchero (bean and sausage or meat stew) it becomes.

### The Sephardim

This was the name given to the Spanish Jews; it is the Hebrew word for Spanish. When the Jews fled from Spain, they took with them many of its vegetables and dishes, including lentils, citron, fried fish, the boiling chicken with the bird's unshed eggs still inside, chicken with olives, and chicken soup with almonds.

**HOLY SWEETMEATS**

At one time, the church employed one tenth of the population, many of them women. In Old Castile and the south, nuns turned to cookie- and sweetmeat-making for charity. Egg whites were used in sherry-making and the left-over yolks given to the convents. The nuns combined these with cheap sugar from the New World to make little natillas (custards) and sweetmeats.

Today, you can still go to closed convents and place your order through the grille or put money on the shelf in a tornador (revolving door) and receive back goodies.

The best-known of these are yemas de San Leandro (egg yolk balls). Christmas brings red quince jellies, coconut truffles, mantecados, polvorones and potato cakes called cubilitos (little cubes). Other delicacies include the almond and cinnamon cream known as bien me sabe (I know it does me good).

*Below: Dried salt cod has been enjoyed in Spain for centuries. In times past, the dried fish was carried across the country by muleteers.*

**FOOD ON THE ROAD**

Spain is a country of mountains, and of fierce regionalism. Nevertheless, it has always had its travellers. The muleteers of León were the equivalent of modern-day lorry drivers, criss-crossing Spain with their load of salt cod and news. They had their own recipe, bacalao ajo arriero (dry, hard fish rehydrated in a pot with oil and garlic), which is now often transformed into a Christmas brandade or into a tomato-based dish.

Tourism is not a new phenomenon in Spain either. Santiago de Compostella has been a major shrine for pilgrims for a millenium. In the 1550s, at the height of its popularity, up to two million people a year, from all over Europe, walked there south of the mountains on the *camino frances*, or along the coast. Scallop shells were their badge, but in their bags they carried bread and smoked sausage. At the pilgrim monasteries, crowds of up to 1,500 were fed on chickpeas and chard.

Another transient people, the gypsies (with a background in Egypt and India) arrived in the 1450s. They settled in Andalusia where they took up the jobs left vacant by the Moors and Jews. They also annexed the folklore of the south and became the smugglers and bandits of the 19th century. Their contribution to the Spanish cuisine was an element of improvisation in food, instead of traditional long-cooked stews.

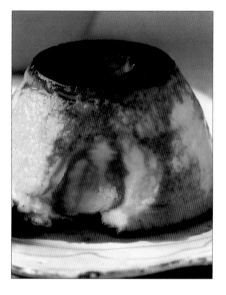

*Above (left and right): The tradition of sweet cookies and custard desserts was once the province of Spanish nuns, who made and sold them for charity.*

**FOODS FROM NEW LANDS**

The introduction of new foods from America after 1492 changed the Mediterranean diet for ever. Spain was transformed from being a bean, grain and meat-eating country, into a place where vegetables were widely enjoyed. An increase in population followed in Spain and Europe.

Chocolate and chilli peppers quickly became firm favourites in the Spanish kitchen: chocolate as a drink, and chillies as a condiment. Tomatoes were adopted and used in sauces, and beans became a firm fixture at the heart of the Spanish cuisine. Potatoes, however, never displaced the great popularity of chickpeas, and corn was adopted only in Spain's fringes. (Could the reason for this be that tobacco was discovered on the same day – and the Spanish preferred the latter?)

From the opposite direction, the Portuguese returning from China in the early 1500s, brought with them sweet oranges. To this day, oranges are still known as chinas. The resulting orange trees, which now grow in such abundance all over Spain, have dramatically altered the landscape of the east and south coast.

*Right and far right: Spain boasts the longest coastline in Europe and from two oceans come a vast array of fresh seafood, including scampi and sardines.*

## BETWEEN TWO OCEANS

Spain's longest frontiers are water so it is no wonder the Spanish are seafarers. Spain has always looked outward to the Atlantic as well as inward to the Mediterranean. First came shipping salt, whaling and fishing. Later Cádiz and Sevilla provided the ships and stores for "the Empire on which the sun never sets" – a phrase used to describe Spain before it was borrowed by the British Empire. In Spain, *América* refers to Latin America, which was open territory for the *conquistadores* (adventurers) to make their fortune.

### Mediterranean links

Since the Phoenicians first arrived and planted olive trees, Spain has long had links with its Eastern neighbours. In terms of food influences, Spain has given much more than it has received.

A huge range of kitchen skills travelled from Spain to other countries, including Italy and France, largely thanks to the Moorish legacy.

*Below: Chillies came from America and became a widely used condiment in Spanish food and cooking.*

### The Recipes

This book contains over 60 easy-to-follow recipes for every occasion. The tempting selection begins with a wonderful range of soups, from Gazpacho to Sherried Onion Soup with Saffron. There are flavoursome main course dishes such as Seafood Paella and Chicken Casserole with Spiced Figs, as well as a variety of vegetables and salads. Also included is a tasty collection of tantalizing desserts, from cooling ice creams and sorbets to dream desserts made from fruit, cream and chocolate.

This superb introduction to Spanish cooking, will enable you to enjoy delicious classics as well as less well-known dishes that the whole family will love.

*Below: Lemons were brought to Spain by the Moors, while sweet oranges were brought from China by the Portuguese.*

*Below: Spanish olives owe their legacy to the Phoenicians who first planted the trees there hundreds of years ago.*

# SOUPS

*A bowl of delicious smooth, chunky or chilled soup makes an excellent appetizer or light lunch at any time of the year. In this section you will find the world-famous soup Gazpacho, as well as many others, from shellfish soups such as Sopa de Mariscos to meaty broths such as Caldo Gallego.*

# CHILLED AVOCADO SOUP <u>WITH</u> CUMIN

*ANDALUSIA IS HOME TO BOTH AVOCADOS AND GAZPACHO, SO IT IS NOT SURPRISING THAT THIS CHILLED AVOCADO SOUP, WHICH IS ALSO KNOWN AS GREEN GAZPACHO, WAS INVENTED THERE. IN SPAIN, THIS DELICIOUSLY MILD, CREAMY SOUP IS KNOWN AS SOPA DE AGUACATE.*

<u>SERVES FOUR</u>

INGREDIENTS

   3 ripe avocados
   1 bunch spring onions (scallions),
     white parts only, trimmed and
     roughly chopped
   2 garlic cloves, chopped
   juice of 1 lemon
   1.5ml/¼ tsp ground cumin
   1.5ml/¼ tsp paprika
   450ml/¾ pint/scant 2 cups fresh
     chicken stock, cooled, and all
     fat skimmed off
   300ml/½ pint/1¼ cups iced water
   salt and ground black pepper
   roughly chopped fresh flat leaf
     parsley, to serve

**1** Starting half a day ahead, put the flesh of one avocado in a food processor or blender. Add the spring onions, garlic and lemon juice and purée until smooth. Add the second avocado and purée, then the third, with the spices and seasoning. Purée until smooth.

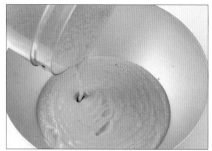

**2** Gradually add the chicken stock. Pour the soup into a metal bowl and chill.

**3** To serve, stir in the iced water, then season to taste with plenty of salt and black pepper. Garnish with chopped parsley and serve immediately.

# GAZPACHO

*This classic chilled soup is deeply rooted in Andalusia. The soothing blend of tomatoes, sweet peppers and garlic is sharpened with sherry vinegar, and enriched with olive oil. Serving it with saucerfuls of garnishes has virtually become a tradition.*

SERVES FOUR

INGREDIENTS

1.3–1.6kg/3–3½lb ripe tomatoes
1 green (bell) pepper, seeded and
  roughly chopped
2 garlic cloves, finely chopped
2 slices stale bread, crusts removed
60ml/4 tbsp extra virgin olive oil
60ml/4 tbsp sherry vinegar
150ml/¼ pint/⅔ cup tomato juice
300ml/½ pint/1¼ cups iced water
salt and ground black pepper
ice cubes, to serve (optional)
For the garnishes
30ml/2 tbsp olive oil
2–3 slices stale bread, diced
1 small cucumber, peeled
  and finely diced
1 small onion, finely chopped
1 red (bell) and 1 green (bell)
  pepper, seeded and finely diced
2 hard-boiled eggs, chopped

**COOK'S TIP**
In Spain, ripe tomatoes are used for salads and very ripe ones for sauces and soups. No further flavouring ingredients are needed. If you cannot find really ripe tomatoes, add a pinch of sugar to sweeten the soup slightly.

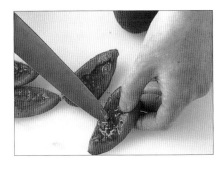

**1** Skin the tomatoes, then quarter them and remove the cores and seeds, saving the juices. Put the pepper in a food processor and process for a few seconds. Add the tomatoes, reserved juices, garlic, bread, oil and vinegar and process. Add the tomato juice and blend to combine.

**2** Season the soup, then pour into a large bowl, cover with clear film (plastic wrap) and chill for at least 12 hours.

**3** Prepare the garnishes. Heat the olive oil in a frying pan and fry the bread cubes for 4–5 minutes until golden brown and crisp. Drain well on kitchen paper, then arrange in a small dish. Place each of the remaining garnishes in separate small dishes.

**4** Just before serving, dilute the soup with the ice-cold water. The consistency should be thick but not too stodgy. If you like, stir a few ice cubes into the soup, then spoon into serving bowls and serve with the garnishes.

# CHILLED ALMOND SOUP WITH GRAPES

*CALLED AJO BLANCO — WHITE GARLIC SOUP — IN SPAIN, THIS IS A CHILLED MOORISH SOUP OF ANCIENT ORIGIN. IT IS A PERFECT BALANCE OF THREE SOUTHERN INGREDIENTS: CRUSHED ALMONDS, GARLIC AND VINEGAR, IN A SMOOTH PURÉE MADE LUSCIOUS WITH OIL.*

SERVES SIX

INGREDIENTS
    115g/4oz stale white bread
    115g/4oz/1 cup blanched
      almonds
    2 garlic cloves, sliced
    75ml/5 tbsp olive oil
    25ml/1½ tbsp sherry vinegar
    salt and ground black pepper
For the garnish
    toasted flaked almonds
    green and black grapes, halved
      and seeded
    chopped fresh chives

**1** Break the bread into a bowl and pour in 150ml/¼ pint/⅔ cup cold water. Leave to soak for about 5 minutes, then squeeze dry.

**2** Put the almonds and garlic in a food processor or blender and process until very finely ground. Add the soaked white bread and process again until thoroughly combined.

**3** Continue to process, gradually adding the oil until the mixture forms a smooth paste. Add the sherry vinegar, followed by 600ml/1 pint/2½ cups cold water and process until the mixture is smooth.

**4** Transfer the soup to a bowl and season with plenty of salt and pepper, adding a little more water if the soup is very thick. Cover with clear film (plastic wrap) and chill for at least 2 hours.

**5** Ladle the soup into bowls. Scatter the almonds, halved grapes and chopped chives over to garnish.

**COOK'S TIP**
To accentuate the flavour of the almonds, dry roast them in a frying pan until they are lightly browned before grinding them. This will produce a slightly darker soup.

# SHERRIED ONION SOUP <u>WITH</u> SAFFRON

*THE SPANISH COMBINATION OF ONIONS, SHERRY AND SAFFRON GIVES THIS PALE YELLOW SOUP A BEGUILING FLAVOUR THAT IS PERFECT FOR THE OPENING COURSE OF A MEAL. THE ADDITION OF GROUND ALMONDS TO THICKEN THE SOUP GIVES IT A WONDERFUL TEXTURE AND FLAVOUR.*

<u>SERVES FOUR</u>

INGREDIENTS
  40g/1½oz/3 tbsp butter
  2 large yellow onions, thinly sliced
  1 small garlic clove, finely chopped
  pinch of saffron threads (0.05g)
  50g/2oz blanched almonds, toasted
    and finely ground
  750ml/1¼ pints/3 cups chicken
    or vegetable stock
  45ml/3 tbsp fino sherry
  2.5ml/½ tsp paprika
  salt and ground black pepper
To garnish
  30ml/2 tbsp flaked or slivered
    almonds, toasted
  chopped fresh parsley

**1** Melt the butter in a heavy pan over a low heat. Add the onions and garlic, stirring to ensure that they are thoroughly coated in the melted butter, then cover the pan and cook very gently, stirring frequently, for about 20 minutes, or until the onions are soft and golden yellow.

**2** Add the saffron threads to the pan and cook, uncovered, for 3–4 minutes, then add the finely ground almonds and cook, stirring the ingredients constantly, for a further 2–3 minutes.

**3** Pour in the chicken or vegetable stock and sherry into the pan and stir in 5ml/1 tsp salt and the paprika. Season with plenty of black pepper. Bring to the boil, then lower the heat and simmer gently for about 10 minutes.

**4** Pour the soup into a food processor and process until smooth, then return it to the rinsed pan. Reheat slowly, without allowing the soup to boil, stirring occasionally. Taste for seasoning, adding more salt and pepper if required.

**5** Ladle the soup into heated bowls, garnish with the toasted flaked or slivered almonds and a little chopped fresh parsley and serve immediately.

**VARIATION**
This soup is also delicious served chilled. Use olive oil rather than butter, add a little more chicken or vegetable stock to make a slightly thinner soup, then leave to cool and chill for at least 4 hours. Just before serving, taste for seasoning. (Chilled soups need more seasoning than hot ones.) Float one or two ice cubes in each bowl, then garnish with almonds and parsley and serve immediately.

# CATALAN BROAD BEAN AND POTATO SOUP

*HABAS ARE FRESH BROAD BEANS, AND ARE A GREAT DEAL NICER THAN THE DRIED VARIETY, KNOWN AS FAVAS. THE WORD HAS VANISHED FROM THE SPANISH DICTIONARY AND THE RATHER INDIGESTIBLE DRIED BEAN HAS ALL BUT DISAPPEARED AS WELL. THIS FRESH SOUP USES A MODERN HERB TOO — CORIANDER IS NOT A COMMON SPANISH INGREDIENT, BUT IT ADDS A DELICIOUS FLAVOUR.*

SERVES FOUR

INGREDIENTS

30ml/2 tbsp olive oil
2 onions, chopped
3 large floury potatoes, peeled
  and diced
450g/1lb fresh shelled broad
  (US fava) beans
1.75 litres/3 pints/7½ cups
  vegetable stock
1 bunch fresh coriander (cilantro),
  roughly chopped
150ml/¼ pint/⅔ cup single
  (light) cream, plus a little extra,
  to garnish
salt and ground black pepper

**1** Heat the oil in a large pan and fry the onions, stirring, for 5 minutes until soft. Add the potatoes, most of the beans (reserving a few for the garnish) and the stock, and bring to the boil. Simmer for 5 minutes, then add the coriander and simmer for a further 10 minutes.

**2** Blend the soup in batches in a food processor or blender, then return to the rinsed pan.

**3** Stir in the cream, season, and bring to a simmer. Serve garnished with coriander, beans and cream.

# SOPA CASTILIANA

*This rich, dark garlic soup, from central Spain, divides people into two groups. You either love it or hate it. The pitiless sun beats down on La Mancha, one of the poorest regions of Spain, and the local soup has harsh, strong tastes to match the climate. Poaching a whole egg in each bowl just before serving transforms the soup into a meal.*

SERVES FOUR

INGREDIENTS
    30ml/2 tbsp olive oil
    4 large garlic cloves, peeled
    4 slices stale country bread
    20ml/4 tbsp paprika
    1 litre/1¾ pints/4 cups beef stock
    1.5ml/¼ tsp ground cumin
    4 free-range (farm-fresh) eggs
    salt and ground black pepper
    chopped fresh parsley, to garnish

**VARIATION**
If you prefer, you can simply whisk
the eggs into the hot soup.

**1** Preheat the oven to 230°C/450°F/
Gas 8. Heat the olive oil in a large pan.
Add the whole peeled garlic cloves and
cook until they are golden, then remove
and set aside. Fry the slices of bread in
the oil until golden, then set these aside.

**2** Add 15ml/1 tbsp of the paprika to the
pan, and fry for a few seconds. Stir in
the beef stock, cumin and remaining
paprika, then add the reserved garlic,
crushing the cloves with the back of a
wooden spoon. Season to taste, then
cook for about 5 minutes.

**3** Break up the slices of fried bread
into bitesize pieces and stir them into
the soup. Ladle the soup into four
ovenproof bowls. Carefully break an
egg into each bowl of soup and place
in the oven for about 3 minutes,
until the eggs are set. Sprinkle the
soup with chopped fresh parsley and
serve immediately.

# SOPA DE MARISCOS

*THIS HEARTY SEAFOOD SOUP CONTAINS ALL THE COLOURS AND FLAVOURS OF THE MEDITERRANEAN. IT IS SUBSTANTIAL ENOUGH TO SERVE AS A MAIN COURSE, BUT CAN ALSO BE DILUTED WITH A LITTLE WHITE WINE AND WATER, TO MAKE AN ELEGANT APPETIZER FOR SIX.*

SERVES FOUR

INGREDIENTS

675g/1½lb raw prawns (shrimp),
  in the shell
900ml/1½pints/3¾ cups cold water
1 onion, chopped
1 celery stick, chopped
1 bay leaf
45ml/3 tbsp olive oil
2 slices stale bread, crusts removed
1 small onion, finely chopped
1 large garlic clove, chopped
2 large tomatoes, halved
½ large green (bell) pepper,
  finely chopped
500g/1¼lb cockles (small clams)
  or mussels, cleaned
juice of 1 lemon
45ml/3 tbsp chopped fresh parsley
5ml/1 tsp paprika
salt and ground black pepper

**COOK'S TIP**
Good fish and shellfish dishes are normally based on proper fish stock (including the juices saved from opening mussels). This is equivalent to the French *court bouillon*, and takes 30 minutes' simmering. The method used here is one of the quickest, because the prawn heads come off neatly, and the rest of the shells are simply added as they are removed.

**1** Pull the heads off the prawns and put them in a pan with the cold water. Add the onion, celery and bay leaf and simmer for 20–25 minutes.

**2** Peel the prawns, adding the shells to the stock as you go along.

**3** Heat the oil in a wide, deep flameproof casserole and fry the bread slices quickly, then reserve them. Fry the onion until it is soft, adding the garlic towards the end.

**4** Scoop the seeds out of the tomatoes and discard. Chop the flesh and add to the casserole with the green pepper. Fry briefly, stirring occasionally.

**5** Strain the stock into the casserole and bring to the boil. Check over the cockles or mussels, discarding any that are open or damaged.

**6** Add half the cockles or mussels to the stock. When open, use a slotted spoon to transfer some of them out on to a plate. Remove the mussels or cockles from the shells and discard the shells. (You should end up having discarded about half of the shells.) Meanwhile, repeat the process to cook the remaining cockles or mussels.

**7** Return the cockles or mussels to the soup and add the prawns. Add the bread, torn into little pieces, and the lemon juice and chopped parsley.

**8** Season to taste with paprika, salt and pepper and stir gently to dissolve the bread. Serve at once in soup bowls, providing a plate for the empty shells.

# FISH SOUP <u>WITH</u> ORANGE

*THE OLD NAME FOR THIS SOUP IS* SOPA CACHORREÑA — *SEVILLE ORANGE SOUP — AND IT IS GOOD SERVED POST-CHRISTMAS, WHEN BITTER SEVILLE ORANGES ARE IN SEASON. IT HAS A BEAUTIFUL ORANGE COLOUR. THE FISH USED IS NORMALLY SMALL HAKE, BUT ANY WHITE FISH IS SUITABLE.*

**2** Heat the oil in a large flameproof casserole over a high heat. Smash the garlic cloves with the flat of a knife and fry until they are well-coloured. Discard them and turn down the heat. Fry the onion gently until it is softened, adding the tomato halfway through.

**3** Strain in the hot fish stock (adding the orange spiral as well if you wish) and bring back to the boil. Add the potatoes to the pan and cook them for about 5 minutes.

**4** Add the fish pieces to the soup, a few at a time, without letting it go off the boil. Cook for about 15 minutes. Add the squeezed orange juice and lemon juice, if using, and the paprika, with salt and pepper to taste. Serve in bowls, garnished with a little parsley.

SERVES SIX

INGREDIENTS
　1kg/2¼lb small hake or whiting,
　　whole but cleaned
　1.2 litres/2 pints/5 cups water
　4 bitter oranges or 4 sweet oranges
　　and 2 lemons
　30ml/2 tbsp olive oil
　5 garlic cloves, unpeeled
　1 large onion, finely chopped
　1 tomato, peeled, seeded
　　and chopped
　4 small potatoes, cut into rounds
　5ml/1 tsp paprika
　salt and ground black pepper
　15–30ml/1–2 tbsp finely chopped
　　fresh parsley, to garnish

**1** Fillet the fish and cut each fillet into three, reserving all the trimmings. Put the fillets on a plate, salt lightly and chill. Put the trimmings in a pan, add the water and a spiral of orange rind. Bring to a simmer, skim, then cover and cook gently for 30 minutes.

# CALDO GALLEGO

*THIS CLASSIC GALICIAN SOUP FEATURES SALT PORK AND BEANS WITH YOUNG TURNIP TOPS, ALTHOUGH PURPLE SPROUTING BROCCOLI MAKES A PRETTY SUBSTITUTE. MAKE THE SOUP AHEAD OF TIME, THEN LET THE FLAVOURS BLEND. YOU WILL NEED TO START MAKING THE SOUP AT LEAST A DAY IN ADVANCE.*

SERVES SIX

INGREDIENTS
   150g/5oz/⅔ cup haricot beans,
      soaked overnight in cold water
      and drained
   1kg/2¼lb smoked gammon (cured
      or smoked ham) hock
   3 potatoes, quartered
   3 small turnips, sliced in rounds
   150g/5oz purple sprouting broccoli
   salt and ground black pepper

**1** Put the drained beans and gammon into a casserole and cover with 2 litres/3½ pints/8 cups water. Slowly bring to the boil, skim off any scum, then turn down the heat and cook gently, covered, for about 1¼ hours.

**2** Drain, reserving the broth. Return the broth to the casserole and add the potatoes, turnips and drained beans.

**3** Meanwhile, strip all the gammon off the bone and return the bone to the broth. Discard the rind, fat and gristle and chop half the meat coarsely. Reserve the remaining meat for another recipe.

**4** Add the chopped meat to the casserole. Discard the hard stalks from the broccoli and add the leaves and florets to the broth. Simmer for 10 minutes. Season generously with pepper, then remove the bone and leave the soup to stand for at least half a day.

**5** To serve, reheat the soup, add a little more seasoning if necessary, and ladle into soup bowls.

**COOK'S TIP**
The leftover gammon can be chopped into bitesize pieces and added to rice or vegetable dishes, or tortillas.

# VEGETABLES
# AND SALADS

*Vegetable dishes are very versatile and can be eaten*

*as tapas or as a main course or side dish.*

*Simple ingredients are cleverly paired to show off*

*their qualities to perfection. The salad dishes*

*included here are typical of Spain's attitude to*

*cooking, using fresh, local, seasonal ingredients.*

# STUFFED TOMATOES AND PEPPERS

*COLOURFUL PEPPERS AND TOMATOES MAKE PERFECT CONTAINERS FOR A SIMPLE RICE, NUT AND HERB STUFFING. THE VEGETABLES BECOME DELICIOUSLY SWEET AND JUICY WHEN BAKED. SERVE TOMATES Y PIMIENTAS RELLENOS AS A SUBSTANTIAL STARTER OR A SUPPER DISH.*

**3** Halve the peppers, leaving the cores intact. Scoop out the seeds. Brush the peppers with 15ml/1 tbsp of the oil.

**4** Fry the onions and garlic in 30ml/ 2 tbsp oil. Stir in most of the almonds. Add the rice, tomato pulp, drained raisins, mint and 30ml/2 tbsp parsley. Season well, then spoon the mixture into the vegetable cases.

**5** Bake uncovered for 20 minutes. Finely chop the remaining almonds and parsley in a food processor and sprinkle over the top. Drizzle with 15–30ml/ 1–2 tbsp olive oil. Return to the oven and bake for a further 20 minutes, or until turning golden. Serve, garnished with more chopped parsley if wished.

**VARIATION**

Small aubergines (eggplant) or large courgettes (zucchini) are also good stuffed. Scoop out the centres, then oil the vegetable cases and bake for about 15 minutes. Chop the centres, fry to soften and add to the stuffing mixture, then fill and bake as for the peppers and tomatoes.

SERVES FOUR

INGREDIENTS
    2 large tomatoes
    1 green (bell) pepper
    1 yellow or orange (bell) pepper
    75ml/5 tbsp olive oil
    2 onions, finely chopped
    2 garlic cloves, finely chopped
    75g/3 oz/¾ cup almonds, chopped
    175g/6oz/1½ cups cooked rice, or
        75g/3oz/scant ½ cup long grain
        rice, cooked and drained
    30ml/2 tbsp Malaga raisins or
        muscatels, soaked in hot water
    30ml/2 tbsp chopped fresh mint
    45ml/3 tbsp chopped fresh flat
        leaf parsley
    salt and ground pepper

**1** Preheat the oven to 190ºC/375ºF/ Gas 5. Cut the tomatoes in half and scoop out the pulp and seeds.

**2** Put the tomato halves on kitchen paper with the cut sides down and leave to drain. Roughly chop the centres and seeds and place in a bowl.

# STEWED AUBERGINE

*THE ARABS INTRODUCED THIS STRANGE VEGETABLE-FRUIT TO ANDALUSIA, WHERE IT WAS COOKED WITH THE ARAB FLAVOURINGS OF CUMIN AND GARLIC. LATER, DISHES SIMILAR TO FRENCH RATATOUILLE BECAME POPULAR. THIS IS A MODERN VERSION OF BERENJENA GUISADA, WITH RED WINE.*

SERVES FOUR

INGREDIENTS
  1 large aubergine (eggplant)
  60–90ml/4–6 tbsp olive oil
  2 shallots, thinly sliced
  4 tomatoes, quartered
  2 garlic cloves, thinly sliced
  60ml/4 tbsp red wine
  30ml/2 tbsp chopped fresh parsley,
    plus extra to garnish
  30–45ml/2–3 tbsp virgin olive oil
    (if serving cold)
  salt and ground black pepper

**1** Slice the aubergine into 1cm/½in rounds. Place them in a large colander and sprinkle with 5–10ml/1–2 tsp salt. Leave to drain for 30 minutes.

**2** Rinse the aubergine slices well, then press between several layers of kitchen paper to remove any excess liquid.

**3** Heat 30ml/2 tbsp of the oil in a large frying pan until smoking. Add one layer of aubergine slices and fry, turning once, until golden brown. Remove to a plate covered with kitchen paper. Heat more oil and fry the second batch in the same way.

**4** Heat 15ml/1 tbsp of oil in a pan and cook the shallots for 5 minutes until golden. Cut the aubergine into strips. Add, with the tomatoes, garlic and wine. Cover and simmer for 30 minutes.

**5** Stir in the parsley, and check the seasonings. Sprinkle with a little more parsley and serve hot. To serve cold, dribble a little virgin olive oil over the dish before it goes on the table.

**COOK'S TIP**
Be sure to heat the oil before adding the aubergine slices and do not be tempted to add more oil once the aubergines are cooking. They will absorb cold oil, resulting in a greasy dish.

# MENESTRA

*This vegetable dish, which contains an assortment of young, new vegetables, is eaten all along the northern coast of Spain to celebrate the arrival of spring. Choose by eye, keeping the quantities in proportion, and paying careful attention to the cooking time each vegetable requires to stay just crisp.*

SERVES SIX

INGREDIENTS

15ml/1 tbsp olive oil
115g/4oz streaky (fatty) bacon
  lardons or diced pancetta
1 onion, chopped
3 garlic cloves, finely chopped
90ml/6 tbsp chopped fresh parsley
175ml/6fl oz/¾ cup dry white wine
150g/5oz green beans
200g/7oz bunched young carrots
6 small new best potatoes, scrubbed
300ml/10fl oz/1¼ cups
  chicken stock
1 corn cob, kernels removed
  (optional)
200g/7oz/2 cups peas
50g/2oz mangetout (snow peas)
salt and ground black pepper
2 hard-boiled eggs, chopped,
  to garnish

**VARIATION**
Change the vegetables at will – the stalk end of asparagus, for example, is excellent. But don't vary the amount of liquid used in the casserole, or the sauce will become watery.

**1** Heat the oil in a small flameproof casserole and fry the bacon or pancetta over a gentle heat for about 5 minutes, or until it crisps. Remove with a slotted spoon and reserve. Add the onion to the casserole and cook in the bacon fat until softened, adding the garlic towards the end.

**2** Remove the cooked onion to a food processor, add 30ml/2 tbsp of the chopped parsley and purée with a little of the white wine.

**3** Meanwhile prepare all the vegetables. Cut the beans into short lengths, and the carrots to the same size.

**4** Bring a pan of salted water to the boil and add the potatoes. Cook for about 10 minutes. Add the carrots to the pan of potatoes, and cook for a further 5 minutes.

**5** Meanwhile, return the bacon to the casserole and add the stock. Put in the beans, sweetcorn and peas and lay the mangetout over the top. Half cover the casserole and leave to simmer for 5–10 minutes, until the vegetables are just cooked.

**6** Drain the potatoes and carrots and add them to the casserole.

**7** Add the rest of the wine and the onion purée to the casserole, warming the liquid and turning the vegetables gently with a wooden spoon. Check the seasoning, adding more if necessary, and serve with the juices. Garnish with chopped egg and the remaining parsley.

**VARIATION**
This dish can also be made with tender meats such as lamb and veal with various combinations of new vegetables. Good combinations include lamb with artichokes and sherry, and veal with carrots and peas. Chop the meat and fry before adding to the casserole with the vegetables for further cooking.

# PISTO MANCHEGO

*A RICH-FLAVOURED AND SIMPLE SUMMER VEGETABLE DISH, FROM THE POOREST AND HOTTEST PART OF SPAIN, LA MANCHA. IT MAY BE EATEN HOT, ALONE OR WITH SUCH THINGS AS FRIED HAM AND EGGS. IT ALSO MAKES A SUBSTANTIAL SALAD, OFTEN WITH CANNED TUNA, OR HARD-BOILED EGGS.*

SERVES FOUR

INGREDIENTS
  45–60ml/3–4 tbsp olive oil
  2 Spanish onions, thinly sliced
  3 garlic cloves, finely chopped
  3 large green (bell) peppers,
    seeded and chopped
  3 large courgettes (zucchini),
    thinly sliced
  5 large ripe tomatoes or 800g/
    1¾lb canned tomatoes,
    with juice
  60ml/4 tbsp chopped fresh parsley
  2 hard-boiled eggs (optional)
  30–45ml/2–3 tbsp virgin olive oil
    (if serving cold)
  salt and ground black pepper

**1** Heat the oil in a large heavy pan or flameproof casserole and cook the onions and garlic gently, until soft.

**2** Add the peppers, courgettes and tomatoes. Season and cook gently for 20 minutes until the flavours blend.

**3** Stir in 30ml/2 tbsp parsley and serve hot, if wished, topped with chopped hard-boiled egg, if using, and more parsley. To serve cold, check the seasoning, adding more if needed, and sprinkle with a little virgin olive oil before adding the garnish.

# ESCALIVADA

*The Catalan name of this celebrated dish means "baked over embers" and, like many other barbecue dishes, it transfers very successfully to the oven. Cooking the vegetables in this way brings out their flavour magnificently.*

SERVES FOUR

INGREDIENTS
    2–3 courgettes (zucchini)
    1 large fennel bulb
    1 Spanish onion
    2 large red (bell) peppers
    450g/1lb butternut squash
    6 whole garlic cloves, unpeeled
    75ml/5 tbsp olive oil
    juice of ½ lemon
    pinch of cumin seeds, crushed
    4 sprigs fresh thyme
    4 medium tomatoes
    salt and ground black pepper

**1** Preheat the oven to 220°C/425°F/ Gas 7. Cut the courgettes lengthways into four pieces. Cut the fennel into similar-sized wedges. Slice the onion lengthways into chunks. Halve and seed the peppers, and slice thickly lengthways. Cut the squash into thick chunks. Smash the garlic cloves with the flat of a knife, but leave the skins on.

**2** Choose a roasting pan into which all the vegetables will fit in one layer. Put in all the vegetables except the tomatoes. Mix together the oil and lemon juice. Pour over the vegetables and toss them. Sprinkle with the cumin seeds, salt and pepper and tuck in the thyme sprigs. Roast for 20 minutes.

**3** Gently stir the vegetables in the oil and add the tomatoes. Cook for a further 15 minutes, or until the vegetables are tender and slightly charred around the edges.

**VARIATIONS**
• This is a very easy, pretty dish and you can vary the choice of vegetables according to what is in the market. Baby vegetables are excellent roasted. Tiny fennel, leeks and squash appear seasonally in supermarkets. Judge the roasting time by their volume.
• Aubergines (eggplant) are frequently included in this mixture, and their flavour is delicious, but they turn a slightly unappetizing grey colour when cooked and served plain.

# ORANGE AND RED ONION SALAD WITH CUMIN

*DURING WINTER IN THE SOUTH OF SPAIN, WHEN OTHER SALAD INGREDIENTS ARE IN SHORT SUPPLY, ORANGES OFTEN FORM THE BASIS OF SALADS. IN THIS ENSALADA DE NARANJAS THEY ARE PARTNERED WITH THINLY SLICED RED ONIONS AND BLACK OLIVES, AND FLAVOURED WITH TWO POPULAR MIDDLE EASTERN INGREDIENTS — CUMIN SEEDS AND MINT.*

SERVES SIX

INGREDIENTS
  6 oranges
  2 red onions
  15ml/1 tbsp cumin seeds
  5ml/1 tsp coarsely ground
    black pepper
  15ml/1 tbsp chopped fresh mint
  90ml/6 tbsp olive oil
  salt
  fresh mint sprigs and black olives,
    to garnish

**COOK'S TIP**
It is important to let the salad stand before serving. This allows the flavours to develop and the pungent taste of the onion to soften slightly.

**1** Using a sharp knife, slice the oranges thinly, working over a bowl to catch any juice. Then, holding each orange slice in turn over the bowl, cut round the middle fleshy section with scissors to remove the peel and pith. Reserve the juice. Slice the two red onions thinly and separate the rings.

**2** Arrange the orange and onion slices in layers in a shallow dish, sprinkling each layer with cumin seeds, pepper, mint, olive oil and salt. Pour in the reserved orange juice. Leave to marinate in a cool place for about 2 hours. Just before serving, scatter with the mint sprigs and black olives.

# MIXED SALAD WITH OLIVES AND CAPERS

*COLOURFUL SALADS START MANY SUMMER MEALS IN SPAIN, AND ARE A COMMUNAL AFFAIR. THE BOWL IS PUT IN THE CENTRE OF THE TABLE AND EVERYONE HELPS THEMSELVES, WITH A FORK.*

SERVES FOUR

INGREDIENTS
  4 large tomatoes
  ½ cucumber
  1 bunch spring onions (scallions)
  1 bunch watercress or rocket
    (arugula), washed
  8 pimiento-stuffed olives
  30ml/2 tbsp drained pickled capers
For the dressing
  1 garlic clove, finely chopped
  30ml/2 tbsp red wine vinegar
  5ml/1 tsp paprika
  2.5ml/½ tsp ground cumin
  75ml/5 tbsp virgin olive oil
  salt and ground black pepper

**COOK'S TIP**
In Spain, tomatoes are always used when red and ripe. Firm tomatoes should be used in salads and soft ones in sauces.

**1** To peel the tomatoes, place them in a heatproof bowl, pour over boiling water to cover and leave to stand for 1 minute. Lift out with a slotted spoon and plunge into a bowl of cold water. Leave for 1 minute, then drain. Slip off the skins and dice the flesh finely. Put in a salad bowl.

**2** Peel the cucumber, dice finely and add to the tomatoes. Trim and chop half the spring onions, and add to the bowl.

**3** Toss the vegetables together, then break the watercress or rocket into small sprigs. Add to the tomato mixture, with the olives and capers.

**4** Make the dressing. Crush the garlic to a paste with a little salt, using the flat of a knife. Put in a bowl and mix in the vinegar and spices. Whisk in the oil and taste for seasoning. Dress the salad, and serve garnished with the remaining spring onions.

# FISH AND SHELLFISH

*Spain is bordered by two oceans hosting the widest*
*range of fish in the world, and seafood is one of*
*the glories of Spanish cooking. This chapter includes*
*an array of colourful salads and delightful*
*appetizers, while simple combinations, with lemon,*
*tomato or potatoes, and hearty stews make*
*delicious main courses.*

# SARDINES EN ESCABECHE

*THE ARABS INVENTED MARINADES AS A MEANS OF PRESERVING POULTRY, MEAT AND GAME, AND ESCABECHE MEANS "ACID" IN ARABIC. IN SPAIN THIS METHOD WAS ENTHUSIASTICALLY ADOPTED AS A MEANS OF KEEPING FISH FRESH. THE FISH ARE ALWAYS FRIED FIRST AND THEN STORED IN VINEGAR.*

**3** Heat the olive oil in a frying pan and fry the sardines for 2–3 minutes on each side. With a metal spatula, remove the fish from the pan to a plate and allow to cool, then pack them in a single layer in a large shallow dish.

**4** To make the marinade, add the olive oil to the oil remaining in the frying pan. Fry the onion and garlic gently for 5–10 minutes until soft and translucent, stirring occasionally. Add the bay leaves, cloves, chilli and paprika, with pepper to taste. Fry, stirring frequently, for another 1–2 minutes.

SERVES TWO TO FOUR

INGREDIENTS
    12–16 sardines, cleaned
    seasoned plain (all-purpose) flour,
        for dusting
    30ml/2 tbsp olive oil
    roasted red onion, green (bell) pepper
        and tomatoes, to garnish
For the marinade
    90ml/6 tbsp olive oil
    1 onion, sliced
    1 garlic clove, crushed
    3–4 bay leaves
    2 cloves
    1 dried red chilli, seeded
        and chopped
    5ml/1 tsp paprika
    120ml/4fl oz/½ cup wine
        or sherry vinegar
    120ml/4fl oz/½ cup white wine
    salt and ground black pepper

**1** Using a sharp knife, cut the heads off the sardines and split each of them along the belly. Turn the fish over so that the backbone is uppermost. Press down along the backbone to loosen it, then carefully lift out the backbone and as many of the remaining little bones as possible.

**2** Close the sardines up again and dust them with seasoned flour.

**5** Stir in the vinegar, wine and a little salt. Allow to bubble up, then pour over the sardines. The marinade should cover the fish completely. When the fish is cool, cover and chill overnight or for up to three days. Serve the sardines and their marinade, garnished with the onion, pepper and tomatoes.

**VARIATION**
Other oily fish such as herrings or sprats (small whitebait) are very good prepared in this way. White fish can also be used.

# SKATE WITH BITTER SALAD LEAVES

*THIS DISH IS POPULAR IN GALICIA, WHICH IS FAMOUS FOR BOTH ITS SKATE AND ITS WATERCRESS.*
*SKATE HAS A DELICIOUS SWEET FLAVOUR, ENHANCED HERE BY ORANGE. IT CONTRASTS WELL WITH*
*ANY BITTER LEAVES — BUY A BAG OF MIXED SALAD LEAVES FOR CONTRASTING TEXTURES AND FLAVOURS.*

### SERVES FOUR

### INGREDIENTS

800g/1¾lb skate wings
15ml/1 tbsp white wine vinegar
4 black peppercorns
1 fresh thyme sprig
175g/6oz bitter salad leaves,
  such as frisée, rocket (arugula),
  radicchio, escarole, lamb's lettuce
  (mâche) and watercress
1 orange
2 tomatoes, peeled, seeded
  and diced
For the dressing
15ml/1 tbsp white wine vinegar
45ml/3 tbsp extra virgin olive oil
1 bunch spring onions (scallions),
  whites finely chopped
salt, paprika and black pepper
crusty bread, to serve

**1** Put the skate wings into a large shallow pan, cover with cold water and add the vinegar, peppercorns and thyme. Bring to the boil, then poach gently for 8–10 minutes, until the flesh comes away easily from the bones.

**2** Make the dressing. Whisk together the vinegar, oil and spring onions and season with salt, paprika and pepper.

**3** Put the salad leaves in a large bowl, pour over the dressing and toss well. Remove the rind from the orange using a zester, then peel it, removing all the pith. Slice into thin rounds.

**4** Flake the fish, discarding the bones, and add to the salad. Add a pinch of zest, the orange slices and tomatoes, toss gently and serve with bread.

# BAKED TROUT WITH RICE, TOMATOES AND NUTS

*Trout is very popular in Spain, particularly in the North, where it is fished in many rivers. Here is a modern recipe for* trucha rellena, *baked in foil with a rice stuffing in which sun-dried tomatoes have been used in place of the more traditional chillies.*

SERVES FOUR

INGREDIENTS

2 fresh trout, about 500g/1¼ lb each
75g/3oz/¾ cup mixed unsalted
  almonds, pine nuts or hazelnuts
25ml/1½ tbsp olive oil, plus extra
  for drizzling
1 small onion, finely chopped
10ml/2 tsp grated fresh root ginger
175g/6oz/1½ cups cooked white
  long grain rice
4 tomatoes, peeled and very
  finely chopped
4 sun-dried tomatoes in oil, drained
  and chopped
30ml/2 tbsp chopped fresh tarragon
2 fresh tarragon sprigs
salt and ground black pepper
dressed green salad leaves,
  to serve

**1** Preheat the oven to 190°C/375°F/ Gas 5. If the trout is unfilleted, use a sharp knife to fillet it. Remove any tiny bones remaining in the cavity using a pair of tweezers.

**2** Spread out the nuts in a shallow tin (pan) and bake for 3–4 minutes until golden brown, shaking the tin occasionally. Chop the nuts roughly.

**3** Heat the olive oil in a small frying pan and fry the onion for 3–4 minutes until soft and translucent. Stir in the grated ginger, cook for a further 1 minute, then spoon into a mixing bowl.

**4** Stir the rice, chopped tomatoes, sun-dried tomatoes, toasted nuts and tarragon into the onion mixture. Season the stuffing well.

**5** Place the trout on individual large pieces of oiled foil and spoon the stuffing into the cavities. Add a sprig of tarragon and a drizzle of olive oil or oil from the sun-dried tomatoes.

**6** Fold the foil over to enclose each trout completely, and put the parcels in a large roasting pan. Bake for about 20 minutes or until the fish is just tender. Cut the fish into thick slices. Serve with the salad leaves.

**COOK'S TIP**
You will need about 75g/3oz/¾ cup of uncooked rice to produce 175g/6oz/ 1½ cups cooked rice.

# TRUCHAS A LA NAVARRA

*TRADITIONALLY, THE TROUT WOULD HAVE COME FROM MOUNTAIN STREAMS AND BEEN STUFFED AND WRAPPED IN LOCALLY CURED HAM. ONE OF THE BEAUTIES OF THIS METHOD IS THAT THE SKINS COME OFF IN ONE PIECE, LEAVING THE SUCCULENT, MOIST FLESH TO BE EATEN WITH THE CRISPED, SALT HAM.*

SERVES FOUR

INGREDIENTS

4 brown or rainbow trout, about
  250g/9oz each, cleaned
16 thin slices Serrano ham, about
  200g/7oz
50g/2oz/¼ cup melted butter, plus
  extra for greasing
salt and ground black pepper
buttered potatoes, to
  serve (optional)

**1** Extend the belly cavity of each trout, cutting up one side of the backbone. Slip a knife behind the rib bones to loosen them (sometimes just flexing the fish makes them pop up). Snip these off from both sides with scissors, and season the fish well inside.

**2** Preheat the grill (broiler) to high, with a shelf in the top position. Line a baking tray with foil and butter it.

**3** Working with the fish on the foil, fold a piece of ham into each belly. Use smaller or broken bits of ham for this, and reserve the eight best slices.

**4** Brush each trout with a little butter, seasoning the outside lightly with salt and pepper. Wrap two ham slices round each one, crossways, tucking the ends into the belly. Grill (broil) the trout for 4 minutes, then carefully turn them over with a metal spatula, rolling them across on the belly, so the ham doesn't come loose, and grill for a further 4 minutes.

**5** Serve the trout hot, with any spare butter spooned over the top. Diners should open the trout on their plates, and eat them from the inside, pushing the flesh off the skin.

# GRILLED RED MULLET WITH BAY LEAVES

*RED MULLET ARE CALLED SALMONETES — LITTLE SALMON — IN SPAIN BECAUSE OF THEIR DELICATE, PALE PINK COLOUR. THEY ARE SIMPLE TO COOK ON A BARBECUE, WITH BAY LEAVES FOR FLAVOUR AND A DRIBBLE OF TANGY DRESSING INSTEAD OF A MARINADE.*

**3** To make the dressing, heat the olive oil in a small pan and fry the chopped garlic with the dried chilli. Add the lemon juice and strain the dressing into a small jug (pitcher). Add the chopped parsley and stir to combine.

**4** Serve the mullet on warmed plates, drizzled with the dressing.

### COOK'S TIPS

• Nicknamed the woodcock of the sea, red mullet are one of the fish that are classically cooked uncleaned to give them extra flavour. In this recipe however, the fish are cleaned and herbs are used to add extra flavour to the fish.
• If cooking on a barbecue, light the barbecue well in advance. Before cooking, the charcoal or wood should be grey, with no flames.

### SERVES FOUR

INGREDIENTS
   4 red mullet, about 225–275g/
      8–10oz each, cleaned and descaled
      if cooking under a grill (broiler)
   olive oil, for brushing
   fresh herb sprigs, such as fennel,
      dill, parsley, or thyme
   2–3 dozen fresh or dried bay leaves
For the dressing
   90ml/6 tbsp olive oil
   6 garlic cloves, finely chopped
   ½ dried chilli, seeded and chopped
   juice of ½ lemon
   15ml/1 tbsp parsley

### COOK'S TIP

If you are cooking on the barbecue, the fish do not need to be scaled.

**1** Prepare the barbecue or preheat the grill (broiler) with the shelf 15cm/6in from the heat source.

**2** Brush each fish with oil and stuff the cavities with the herb sprigs. Brush the grill pan with oil and lay bay leaves across the cooking rack. Place the fish on top and cook for 15–20 minutes until cooked through, turning once.

# PAN-FRIED SOLE WITH LEMON AND CAPERS

*FLAT FISH OF DIFFERENT SORTS ABOUND IN THE MEDITERRANEAN AND ARE USUALLY FRIED SIMPLY AND SERVED WITH LEMON WEDGES TO SQUEEZE OVER THE TOP. INTENSELY FLAVOURED CAPERS, WHICH GROW EXTENSIVELY IN THE BALEARIC ISLANDS, MAKE A PLEASANT TANGY ADDITION.*

SERVES TWO

INGREDIENTS

    30–45ml/2–3 tbsp plain
      (all-purpose) flour
    4 sole, plaice or flounder fillets,
      or 2 whole small flat fish
    45ml/3 tbsp olive oil
    25g/1oz/2 tbsp butter
    60ml/4 tbsp lemon juice
    30ml/2 tbsp pickled capers, drained
    salt and ground black pepper
    fresh flat leaf parsley, to garnish
    lemon wedges, to serve

**COOK'S TIP**

This is a flavourful, and quick, way to serve the fillets of any white fish. The delicate flavour is enhanced by the tangy lemon juice and capers.

**1** Sift the flour on to a plate and season well with salt and ground black pepper. Dip the fish fillets into the flour, to coat evenly on both sides.

**2** Heat the oil and butter in a large shallow pan until foaming. Add the fish fillets and fry over a medium heat for 2–3 minutes on each side.

**3** Lift out the fillets carefully with a metal spatula and place them on a warmed serving platter. Season with salt and ground black pepper.

**4** Add the lemon juice and capers to the pan, heat through and pour over the fish. Garnish with parsley and serve at once with lemon wedges.

# SEA BASS <sup>IN A</sup> SALT CRUST

*Baking fish in a crust of sea salt enhances the flavour and brings out the taste of the sea. It is also the easiest way there is to cook a whole fish. In Spain the gilt-head bream is the fish most often used, but any firm fish, such as grey mullet, striped bass and porgy, can be cooked this way. Break open the crust at the table to release the glorious aroma.*

SERVES FOUR TO SIX

INGREDIENTS

   1 sea bass, about 1kg/2¼lb,
     gutted and scaled
   1 sprig each of fresh fennel,
     rosemary and thyme
   mixed peppercorns
   2kg/4½lb coarse sea salt
   seaweed or samphire, to garnish
     (optional)
   lemon slices, to serve

**COOK'S TIP**

In the Mediterranean, fish in salt are often baked whole and ungutted. But supermarkets elsewhere always sell them gutted, so use the opportunity to add flavourings inside.

**1** Preheat the oven to 240°C/475°F/ Gas 9. Fill the cavity of the sea bass with the fennel, rosemary and thyme sprigs and grind over some of the mixed peppercorns.

**2** Spread half the salt in a shallow baking tray and lay the sea bass on it.

**3** Cover the fish all over with a 1cm/½in layer of salt, pressing it down firmly. Bake for 30 minutes, until the salt coagulates and is beginning to colour.

**4** To serve, leave the fish on the baking tray and garnish with seaweed or samphire, if using. Bring the fish to the table in its salt crust. Use a sharp knife to break open the crust.

**COOK'S TIP**

Once baked, the salt sticks to the fish skin, and brings it off. Scrape back the layer of salt and lift out the top fillet in sections. Snip the backbone with scissors and lift out. Discard the herbs and remove the bottom fillet pieces. Add a lemon slice to each plate.

# BACALAO IN SPICY TOMATO WITH POTATOES

*SALT COD IS A POPULAR INGREDIENT IN SPAIN, NOT JUST A LENTEN NECESSITY. IT IS THE SALT THAT MAKES THE FISH SO CHARACTERFUL, SO DON'T OVERSOAK IT FOR THIS TRADITIONAL BASQUE RECIPE. LOOK OUT FOR A LOIN PIECE, WHICH HAS VERY LITTLE WASTE; IF YOU CAN'T FIND ONE, BUY A LARGER PIECE TO ENSURE YOU HAVE ENOUGH ONCE ANY VERY DRY BITS HAVE BEEN REMOVED.*

SERVES FOUR

INGREDIENTS
400g/14oz salt cod loin, soaked
   in cold water for 24 hours
30ml/2 tbsp olive oil
1 large onion, chopped
2 garlic cloves, finely chopped
1½ green (bell) peppers, seeded
   and chopped
500g/1¼ lb ripe tomatoes, peeled
   and chopped, or a 400g/14oz
   can tomatoes
15ml/1 tbsp tomato purée (paste)
15ml/1 tbsp clear honey
1.5ml/¼ tsp dried thyme
2.5ml/½ tsp cayenne pepper
juice of ½ lemon (optional)
2 potatoes
45ml/3 tbsp stale breadcrumbs
30ml/2 tbsp finely chopped
   fresh parsley
salt and ground black pepper

**1** Drain the salt cod and place in a pan. Pour over water to cover generously and bring to the boil. Remove the pan from the heat as soon as the water boils, then set aside until cold.

**2** Heat the oil in a medium pan. Fry the onion, and add the garlic after 5 minutes. Add the chopped peppers and tomatoes, and cook gently to form a sauce. Stir in the tomato purée, honey, dried thyme, cayenne, black pepper and a little salt. Taste for seasoning: a little lemon juice will make it tangier.

**3** Halve the potatoes lengthways and cut them into slices just thicker than a coin. Drain the fish, reserving the cooking water.

**4** Preheat the grill (broiler) to medium with a shelf 15cm/6in below it. Bring the reserved fish cooking water to the boil and cook the potatoes for about 8 minutes. Do not add extra salt.

**5** Remove the skin and bones from the cod, and pull it into small natural flakes. Spoon one-third of the tomato sauce into a flameproof casserole, top with the potatoes, fish and remaining sauce. Combine the breadcrumbs and parsley and sprinkle over. Heat the dish through under a grill for 10 minutes.

# MACKEREL IN LEMON SAMFAINA

*SAMFAINA IS A SAUCE FROM THE EAST COAST OF SPAIN AND THE COSTA BRAVA. IT SHARES THE SAME INGREDIENTS AS RATATOUILLE AND IS RATHER LIKE A CHUNKY VEGETABLE STEW. THIS VERSION IS PARTICULARLY LEMONY, TO OFFSET THE RICHNESS OF THE MACKEREL.*

SERVES FOUR

INGREDIENTS

2 large mackerel, filleted, or 4 fillets
plain (all-purpose) flour, for dusting
30ml/2 tbsp olive oil
lemon wedges, if serving cold
For the samfaina sauce
1 large aubergine (eggplant)
60ml/4 tbsp olive oil
1 large onion, chopped
2 garlic cloves, finely chopped
1 large courgette (zucchini), sliced
1 red and 1 green (bell) pepper,
   seeded and cut into squares
800g/1¾lb ripe tomatoes,
   roughly chopped
1 bay leaf
salt and ground black pepper

**1** Make the sauce. Peel the aubergine, then cut the flesh into cubes, sprinkle with salt and leave to stand in a colander for 30 minutes.

**2** Heat half the oil in a flameproof casserole large enough to fit the fish. Fry the onion over a medium heat until it colours. Add the garlic, then the courgette and peppers and stir-fry.

**3** Add the tomatoes and bay leaf, partially cover and simmer over the lowest heat, letting the tomatoes just soften without losing their shape.

**4** Rinse off the salt from the aubergine. Using three layers of kitchen paper, squeeze the cubes dry.

**5** Heat the remaining oil in a frying pan until smoking. Put in one handful of aubergine cubes, then the next, stirring with a wooden spoon and cooking over a high heat until the cubes are brown on all sides. Stir into the tomato sauce.

**6** Cut each mackerel fillet into three, and dust the filleted side with flour. Heat the oil in a frying pan over a high heat and put the fish in, floured side down. Fry for 3 minutes until golden. Turn and cook for another 1 minute, then slip the fish into the sauce and simmer, covered, for 5 minutes. Adjust the seasonings before serving.

**COOK'S TIP**
The fish can be served hot or cold. If serving cold, present the mackerel skin-side up, surrounded by vegetables, and garnished with lemon wedges.

# MONKFISH WITH PIMIENTO AND CREAM SAUCE

*THIS RECIPE COMES FROM RIOJA COUNTRY, WHERE A SPECIAL HORNED RED PEPPER GROWS AND IS USED TO MAKE A SPICY SAUCE. HERE, RED PEPPERS ARE USED WITH A LITTLE CHILLI WHILE CREAM MAKES A MELLOW PINK SAUCE. TO DRINK, CHOOSE A MARQUES DE CÁCERES WHITE RIOJA.*

SERVES FOUR

INGREDIENTS

2 large red (bell) peppers
1kg/2¼lb monkfish tail
 or 900g/2lb halibut
plain (all-purpose) flour,
 for dusting
30ml/2 tbsp olive oil
25g/1oz/2 tbsp butter
120ml/4fl oz/½ cup white Rioja
 or dry vermouth
½ dried chilli, seeded and chopped
8 raw prawns (shrimp), in the shell
150ml/¼ pint/⅔ cup double
 (heavy) cream
salt and ground black pepper
fresh flat leaf parsley, to garnish

**1** Preheat the grill (broiler) to high and cook the peppers for 8–12 minutes, turning occasionally, until they are soft, and the skins blackened. Leave, covered, until cool enough to handle. Skin and discard the stalks and seeds. Put the flesh into a blender, strain in the juices and purée.

**2** Cut the monkfish or halibut into eight steaks (freeze the bones for stock). Season well and dust with flour.

**3** Heat the oil and butter in a large frying pan and fry the fish for 3 minutes on each side. Remove to a warm dish.

**4** Add the wine or vermouth and chilli to the pan and stir to deglaze the pan. Add the prawns and cook them briefly, then lift out and reserve.

**5** Boil the sauce to reduce by half, then strain into a small jug (pitcher). Add the cream to the pan and boil briefly to reduce. Return the sauce to the pan, stir in the puréed peppers and check the seasonings. Pour the sauce over the fish and serve garnished with the cooked prawns and parsley.

# CHAR-GRILLED SQUID

*CALAMARES A LA PLANCHA ARE TRADITIONALLY COOKED ON THE HOT GRIDDLE THAT IS AN ESSENTIAL PART OF EVERY SPANISH KITCHEN. THE METHOD IS FAST AND SIMPLE AND REALLY BRINGS OUT THE FLAVOUR OF THE SQUID. THIS DISH IS AN IDEAL FIRST COURSE FOR FOUR PEOPLE, OR CAN BE SERVED ON A BED OF RICE AS A MAIN DISH FOR TWO.*

**3** Heat a ridged griddle pan until hot. Add the body of one of the squid and cook over a medium heat for 2–3 minutes, pressing the squid with a metal spatula to keep it flat. Repeat on the other side. Cook the other squid body in the same way.

**4** Cut the squid bodies into diagonal strips. If serving with rice, arrange the squid strips criss-cross on top. Keep hot.

SERVES TWO TO FOUR

INGREDIENTS
  2 whole cleaned squid, with
    tentacles, about 275g/10oz each
  75ml/5 tbsp olive oil
  30ml/2 tbsp sherry vinegar
  2 fresh red chillies, finely
    chopped
  60ml/4 tbsp dry white wine
  salt and ground black pepper
  hot cooked rice, to serve (optional)
  15–30ml/1–2 tbsp chopped parsley,
    to garnish

**1** Make a lengthways cut down the side of the body of each squid, then open it out flat. Score the flesh on both sides of the bodies in a criss-cross pattern with the tip of a sharp knife. Chop the tentacles into short lengths. Place all the squid pieces in a non-metallic dish.

**2** Whisk together the oil and vinegar in a small bowl. Add salt and pepper to taste, pour over the squid and toss to mix. Cover and leave to marinate for about 1 hour.

**5** Add the chopped tentacles and chillies to the pan and toss over a medium heat for 2 minutes. Stir in the wine, then drizzle over the squid. Garnish with chopped parsley.

# SEAFOOD PAELLA

*THIS IS A GREAT DISH TO SERVE TO GUESTS ON A SPECIAL OCCASION. A SEAFOOD PAELLA ALWAYS LOOKS SPECTACULAR AND A BED OF SCENTED RICE IS THE PERFECT WAY TO DISPLAY A SELECTION OF MARISCOS (SEAFOOD). THIS PARTICULAR PAELLA CONTAINS A MAGNIFICENT COMBINATION OF SQUID, PRAWNS, MUSSELS AND CLAMS AS WELL AS SPICY CHORIZO AND SUCCULENT VEGETABLES.*

SERVES FOUR

INGREDIENTS

    45ml/3 tbsp olive oil
    1 Spanish onion, chopped
    2 large garlic cloves, chopped
    150g/5oz frying chorizo, sliced
    300g/11oz small squid, cleaned
    1 red (bell) pepper, cut into strips
    4 tomatoes, peeled, seeded and
      diced or 200g/7oz can tomatoes
    500ml/17fl oz/2¼ cups chicken
      stock, plus a little extra
    105ml/7 tbsp dry white wine
    200g/7oz/1 cup paella rice
    pinch of saffron threads (0.2g),
      crumbled
    150g/5oz/generous 1 cup peas
    12 large cooked prawns (shrimp),
      in the shell or 8 peeled scampi
      (extra large shrimp)
    450g/1lb fresh mussels, scrubbed
    450g/1lb clams, scrubbed
    4 cooked king prawns (jumbo shrimp)
      or scampi, in the shells
    salt and ground black pepper
    chopped fresh parsley and lemon
      wedges, to garnish

**1** Heat the olive oil in a paella pan or large frying pan, add the onion and garlic and fry until translucent. Add the chorizo and fry until lightly golden.

**2** If the squid are very small, leave them whole, otherwise cut the bodies into rings and the tentacles into pieces. Add the squid to the pan and sauté over a high heat for 2 minutes.

**3** Stir in the pepper and tomatoes and simmer gently for 5 minutes, until the pepper is tender. Pour in the stock and wine, stir well and bring to the boil. Stir in the rice and saffron and season well. Spread the contents evenly over the base of the pan. Bring the liquid back to the boil, then lower the heat and simmer for about 10 minutes.

**4** Gently stir the peas, prawns or scampi, mussels and clams into the rice, then cook for a further 15–20 minutes, until the rice is tender and all the mussels and clams have opened. (Discard any that remain closed.) If the paella seems dry, stir in a little more hot stock.

**5** Remove the pan from the heat and arrange the king prawns or scampi on top. Cover and leave to stand for 5 minutes. Sprinkle the paella with chopped parsley and serve from the pan, accompanied by lemon wedges.

# OCTOPUS STEW

*IN GALICIA, OCTOPUS STEWS ARE PARTICULARLY POPULAR AND A COMMON TAPAS DISH IS A SIMPLE STEW WITH PAPRIKA, SERVED ON LITTLE WOODEN PLATES. HERE THE OCTOPUS IS STEWED WITH TOMATOES AND POTATOES, TO MAKE A SUBSTANTIAL MAIN COURSE. IT IS AN IDEAL MAKE-IN-ADVANCE DISH, BECAUSE OCTOPUS CAN BE TOUGH, AND BENEFITS FROM LONG COOKING TO TENDERIZE IT.*

SERVES FOUR TO SIX

INGREDIENTS

1kg/2¼lb octopus, cleaned
45ml/3 tbsp olive oil
1 large red onion, chopped
3 garlic cloves, finely chopped
30ml/2 tbsp brandy
300ml/½ pint/1¼ cups dry
  white wine
800g/1¾lb ripe plum tomatoes,
  peeled and chopped or 2 × 400g/
  14oz cans chopped tomatoes
1 dried red chilli, seeded
  and chopped
1.5ml/¼ tsp paprika
450g/1lb small new potatoes
15ml/1 tbsp chopped fresh rosemary
15ml/1 tbsp fresh thyme leaves
1.2 litres/2 pints/5 cups fish stock
30ml/2 tbsp chopped fresh flat leaf
  parsley leaves
salt and ground black pepper
rosemary sprigs, to garnish
salad leaves and French bread,
  to serve

**3** Pour the brandy over the octopus and ignite it. When the flames have died down, add the wine, bring to the boil and bubble gently for about 5 minutes. Stir in the chopped tomatoes, with the chilli and paprika, then add the potatoes, rosemary and thyme. Simmer gently for 5 minutes.

**4** Pour in the fish stock and season. Cover and simmer for 20–30 minutes, stirring occasionally, until the octopus and potatoes are tender and the sauce has thickened slightly.

**5** To serve, check the seasoning and stir in the parsley. Garnish with rosemary and accompany with salad and bread.

**COOK'S TIPS**
• Octopus skin can be removed with salted fingers. Large octopus often have scaly rings inside the suckers. Run your fingers down the tentacles to pop out.
• You can make this dish the day before. Simply leave to cool, then chill. To serve, reheat gently, then check the seasoning and stir in the parsley.

**1** Cut the octopus into large pieces, put in a pan and pour over enough cold water to cover. Season with salt, bring to the boil, then lower the heat and simmer for 30 minutes to tenderize it. Drain and cut into bitesize pieces.

**2** Heat the oil in a large shallow pan. Fry the onion until lightly coloured, then add the garlic and fry for 1 minute. Add the octopus and fry for 2–3 minutes, stirring, until coloured.

# MARMITAKO

*This is a traditional fisherman's stew, often made at sea, with meaty tuna steaks.*
*The substantial fish is wonderfully balanced by sweet peppers and cider, all topped*
*by potatoes. It takes its name from the cooking pot, known in France as a "marmite".*
*Traditionally a one-pot dish, it speeds things along to fry the fish separately.*

SERVES FOUR

INGREDIENTS
   60ml/4 tbsp olive oil
   1 onion, chopped
   2 garlic cloves, finely chopped
   3 green (bell) peppers, seeded
      and chopped
   ½ dried hot chilli, seeded
      and chopped
   4 light tuna or bonito steaks,
      about 150g/5oz each
   400g/14oz can tomatoes with juice
   10ml/2 tsp paprika
   3 potatoes, diced
   350ml/12fl oz/1½ cups dry
      (hard) cider
   salt and ground black pepper
   30ml/2 tbsp chopped fresh parsley,
      to garnish

**1** Heat half the oil in a shallow
flameproof casserole big enough to
take the fish. Fry the onion gently until
softened, then add the garlic. Add the
peppers and chilli and stir-fry gently.

**2** Season the fish steaks. Heat the
remaining oil in a frying pan and fry
the fish steaks for 2 minutes on each
side over a high heat. Add the tomatoes
to the casserole and stir-fry briefly.
Add the paprika, then salt and pepper
to taste.

**VARIATION**
Veal steaks or chops can be cooked in
the same way. Fry for 5 minutes on each
side in step 2, then continue as with fish.

**3** Slip the fish steaks into the sauce,
moving the peppers into the spaces
between them. Cover with the potatoes,
pushing them as flat as possible.
Add the cider and bring to a simmer.
Cover and cook very gently for about
45 minutes, or until the potatoes are
done. Check the seasoning, sprinkle
with the chopped parsley and serve
immediately, straight from the casserole.

# POULTRY
# AND GAME BIRDS

*Chicken was once considered a luxury in Spain, and
there are many traditional recipes. Other poultry,
such as duck and turkey, and also game birds are
immensely popular. They may be stuffed with grapes,
marinaded in wine, cooked with mushrooms or served
in delicious sauces.*

# CRUMBED CHICKEN WITH GREEN MAYONNAISE

*PECHUGAS DE POLLO REBOZADAS ARE SOLD READY-PREPARED IN EVERY BUTCHER'S IN THE SOUTH. IDENTICAL TO SCHNITZEL, THESE CRISPY, GOLDEN CHICKEN BREAST PORTIONS SHOW THE JEWISH INFLUENCE ON COOKING IN THE REGION. LEMON WEDGES ARE A POPULAR ACCOMPANIMENT.*

SERVES FOUR

INGREDIENTS

  4 boneless chicken breasts fillets,
    each weighing about 200g/7oz
  juice of 1 lemon
  5ml/1 tsp paprika
  plain (all-purpose) flour,
    for dusting
  1–2 eggs
  dried breadcrumbs, for coating
  about 60ml/4 tbsp olive oil
  salt and ground black pepper
  lemon wedges (optional), to serve
For the mayonnaise
  120ml/4fl oz/½ cup mayonnaise
  30ml/2 tbsp pickled capers, drained
    and chopped
  30ml/2 tbsp chopped fresh parsley

**1** Start a couple of hours ahead, if you can. Skin the chicken breasts. Lay them outside down and, with a sharp knife, cut horizontally, almost through, from the rounded side. Open them up like a book. Press gently, to make a roundish shape, the size of a side plate. Sprinkle with lemon juice and paprika.

**2** Set out three plates. Sprinkle flour over one, seasoning it well. Beat the egg with a little salt and pour into the second. Sprinkle the third with dried breadcrumbs. Dip the breasts first into the flour on both sides, then into the egg, then into the breadcrumbs. Chill the crumbed chicken, if you have time.

**3** Put the mayonnaise ingredients in a bowl and mix well to combine.

**4** Heat the oil in a heavy frying pan over a high heat. Fry the breast portions, two at a time, turning after 3 minutes, until golden on both sides. Add more oil for the second batch if needed. Serve at once, with the mayonnaise and lemon wedges, if using.

# ARROZ <u>CON</u> POLLO

*MANY SPANISH FAMILIES EAT RICE ONCE A WEEK, REFERRING TO IT AS ARROZ UNLESS IT IS PAELLA.*
*RICE WITH CHICKEN IS A CASSEROLE, WITH MORE LIQUID THAN A PAELLA. SEASONAL VEGETABLES*
*ARE INCLUDED AND EVEN PEAS AND SWEETCORN CAN BE USED.*

SERVES FOUR

INGREDIENTS
60ml/4 tbsp olive oil
6 chicken thighs, free-range if
   possible, halved along the bone
5ml/1 tsp paprika
1 large Spanish onion,
   roughly chopped
2 garlic cloves, finely chopped
1 chorizo sausage, sliced
115g/4oz Serrano or cooked ham
   or gammon, diced
1 red (bell) pepper, seeded and
   roughly chopped
1 yellow (bell) pepper, seeded and
   roughly chopped
225g/8oz/1 generous cup paella rice,
   washed and drained
2 large tomatoes, chopped or
   200g/7oz can chopped tomatoes
120ml/4fl oz/½ cup amontillado
   sherry
750ml/1¼ pints/3 cups
   chicken stock
5ml/1 tsp dried oregano or thyme
1 bay leaf
salt and ground black pepper
15 green olives and chopped fresh
   flat leaf parsley, to garnish

**1** Heat the oil in a wide flameproof casserole. Season the chicken pieces with salt and paprika. Fry until nicely brown all over, then reserve on a plate.

**2** Add the onion and garlic to the pan and fry gently until beginning to soften. Add the chorizo and ham or gammon and stir-fry. Add the chopped peppers. Cook until they begin to soften.

**3** Sprinkle in the drained rice and cook, stirring, for 1–2 minutes. Add the tomatoes, sherry, chicken stock and dried herbs and season well. Arrange the chicken pieces deep in the mixture, and tuck in the bay leaf.

**4** Cover and cook over a very low heat for 30–40 minutes, until the chicken and rice are done. Stir, then garnish and serve.

# POLLO A LA ESPAÑOLA

*THIS COLOURFUL CHICKEN DISH IS MADE THROUGHOUT SPAIN IN AN INFINITE NUMBER OF VARIATIONS. CUBED SERRANO HAM CAN REPLACE THE BACON, BUT THE FAT THE LATTER GIVES OFF IS A CONSTANT THEME IN THE SPANISH KITCHEN, SO HELPS TO ADD TO ITS CHARACTER.*

SERVES FOUR

INGREDIENTS
    5ml/1 tsp paprika
    4 free-range or corn-fed
      chicken portions
    45ml/3 tbsp olive oil
    150g/5oz smoked bacon lardons,
      or diced pancetta
    1 large onion, chopped
    2 garlic cloves, finely chopped
    1 green (bell) pepper
    1 red (bell) pepper
    450g/1lb tomatoes or 400g/14oz
      canned tomatoes
    30ml/2 tbsp chopped fresh parsley
    salt and ground black pepper
    boiled rice, to serve (optional)

**1** Rub paprika and salt into the chicken portions. Heat 30ml/2 tbsp oil in a large frying pan. Put in the chicken portions, skin side down, and fry gently.

**2** Heat 15ml/1 tbsp oil in a flameproof casserole and add the bacon or pancetta.

**3** When the bacon or pancetta starts to give off fat, add the chopped onion and garlic, frying very gently until soft.

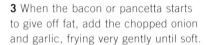

**4** Remove and discard the stalks and seeds from the peppers and roughly chop the flesh. Spoon off a little fat from the chicken pan, then add the peppers, fitting them into the spaces between the chicken portions, and cook gently.

**5** When the onions are soft, stir in the tomatoes and season. Arrange the chicken pieces in the sauce, and stir in the cooked peppers.

**6** Cover the casserole tightly and simmer over a low heat for 15 minutes. Check the seasoning, stir in the chopped parsley and serve with rice, if you like.

# CHICKEN CASSEROLE WITH SPICED FIGS

*THE CATALANS HAVE A REPUTATION FOR SERVING FRUIT WITH POULTRY AND MEAT. FIGS GROW WILD AROUND MANY COUNTRY FARMS AND THE POULTRY FEED ON THE FALLEN FRUIT, SO A DISH COMBINING CHICKEN AND FIGS SEEMS LIKE A NATURAL COMBINATION. HERE POLLO CON HIGOS IS COOKED WITH A BEAUTIFULLY SPICED SAUCE, WHICH GOES PERFECTLY WITH A CATALAN CABERNET SAUVIGNON.*

SERVES FOUR

INGREDIENTS
  50g/2oz bacon lardons or
    pancetta, diced
  15ml/1 tbsp olive oil
  1.3–1.6kg/3–3½lb free-range
    or corn-fed chicken, jointed
    into eight pieces
  120ml/4fl oz/½ cup white wine
  finely pared rind of ½ lemon
  50ml/2fl oz/¼ cup chicken stock
  salt and ground black pepper
  green salad, to serve
For the figs
  150g/5oz/¾ cup granulated sugar
  120ml/4fl oz/½ cup white
    wine vinegar
  1 lemon slice
  1 cinnamon stick
  120ml/4fl oz/½ cup water
  450g/1lb fresh figs

**1** Prepare the figs. Simmer the sugar, vinegar, lemon and cinnamon with the water for 5 minutes. Add the figs and cook for 10 minutes. Remove from the heat and leave to stand for 3 hours.

**2** Fry the bacon or pancetta until golden. Transfer to an ovenproof dish. Add the oil to the pan. Season the chicken, brown on both sides, then transfer to the ovenproof dish.

**3** Preheat the oven to 180°C/350°F/ Gas 4. Drain the figs. Add the wine and lemon rind to the pan and boil until the wine has reduced and is syrupy. Pour over the chicken.

**4** Cook the chicken in the oven, uncovered, for about 20 minutes, then add the figs and chicken stock. Cover and return to the oven for a further 10 minutes. Serve with a green salad.

# POLLO <u>CON</u> LANGOSTINOS

*Chicken with prawns is another gorgeous Catalan dish. The sauce is thickened with a picada of ground toasted almonds, which is more convenient than making a roux with butter and flour at the last moment. This special picada traditionally includes crumbled butter biscuits, which were considered more sophisticated than the bread that normally goes into picada. The sauce is finished with cream and cayenne, as a modern touch – a splendid dinner-party dish. Serve with a glass of Torres Gran Viña Sol.*

SERVES FOUR

INGREDIENTS
    1.3kg/3lb free-range chicken
    75–90ml/5–6 tbsp olive oil
    1 large onion, chopped
    2 garlic cloves, finely chopped
    400g/14oz tomatoes, peeled and
        seeded then chopped or 400g/14oz
        can tomatoes, drained
    1 bay leaf
    150ml/¼ pint/⅔ cup dry white wine
    450g/1lb large raw prawns (shrimp),
        or 16 large shelled prawn tails
    15g/½oz/1 tbsp butter
    30ml/2 tbsp anis spirit, such as
        Ricard or Pernod
    75ml/2½fl oz/⅓ cup double
        (heavy) cream
    1.5ml/¼ tsp cayenne pepper
    salt, paprika and ground
        black pepper
    fresh flat leaf parsley, to garnish
    boiled rice or raw spinach salad,
        to serve
For the *picada*
    25g/1oz/¼ cup blanched almonds
    15g/½oz/1 tbsp butter
    1 garlic clove, finely chopped
    3 Marie, Rich Tea or plain all-butter
        biscuits (cookies), broken
    90ml/6 tbsp chopped fresh parsley

**1** Cut the chicken into eight serving portions, then separate the small fillet from the back of each breast portion. Rub salt and paprika into the chicken.

**2** Heat 30ml/2 tbsp oil in a wide flameproof casserole and fry the onion and garlic until soft. Put in the chicken pieces, skin downwards, and fry over a medium heat, turning until they are golden on all sides.

**3** Meanwhile, make the *picada*. Dry-fry the almonds in a small frying pan, shaking it regularly, until they are just coloured. Transfer them to a blender.

**4** Add 15g/½oz/1 tbsp butter to the pan and gently fry the garlic, then add it to the blender, with the broken biscuits. Reduce the biscuits to crumbs then add the chopped parsley and blend to a purée, adding a little of the wine intended for the casserole.

**5** Add the tomatoes to the casserole, tuck in the bay leaf and cook down to a sauce, stirring occasionally. Pour in the remaining wine, season to taste with salt and ground black pepper, and leave to simmer gently.

**6** Check the shelled prawn tails, if using: if they have a black thread along the back, nick it out with a knife. Heat 15ml/1 tbsp oil and the 15g/½oz/1 tbsp butter in the frying pan and add the prawns. Cook over a medium heat for 2 minutes on each side.

**7** Pour the anis spirit into a ladle and set light to it. Off the heat pour this over the prawns and let it burn off. Stir in the juices from the casserole, then add the pan contents to the casserole.

**8** Remove the bay leaf from the pan and stir in the *picada*, then the cream. Add cayenne to taste and check the seasonings, adding a little more if necessary. Heat through gently and serve garnished with more parsley.

**VARIATIONS**
The classic version of this dish is beef fillet with lobster. Also try veal with scampi, or partridge with large prawns, for equally delicious results.

# ROAST TURKEY WITH BLACK FRUIT STUFFING

*COLUMBUS INTRODUCED TURKEYS FROM AMERICA TO SPAIN, AND AT FIRST THEY WERE COOKED LIKE PEACOCKS — STUFFED, THEN ROASTED INSIDE A PIG'S CAUL. THE SAUSAGEMEAT INSIDE THIS BIRD IS BLACK MORCILLA, AND PRUNES AND RAISINS MAKE IT EVEN MORE SWEET AND FRUITY. THE SAUCE IS FLAVOURED WITH SWEET GRAPE JUICE AND AN INTRIGUING SPLASH OF ANIS.*

SERVES EIGHT

INGREDIENTS

3kg/6½lb bronze or black turkey, weighed without the giblets
60ml/4 tbsp oil
200g/7oz rashers (strips) streaky (fatty) bacon

For the stuffing
45ml/3 tbsp olive oil
1 onion, chopped
2 garlic cloves, finely chopped
115g/4oz fatty bacon lardons
150g/5oz morcilla or black pudding (blood sausage), diced
1 turkey liver, diced
50g/2oz/½ cup Muscatel raisins, soaked in 45ml/3 tbsp anis spirit, such as Ricard, and chopped
115g/4oz ready-to-eat pitted prunes, chopped
50g/2oz/½ cup almonds, chopped
1.5ml/¼ tsp dried thyme
finely grated rind of 1 lemon
freshly grated nutmeg
60ml/4 tbsp chopped fresh parsley
1 large (US extra large) egg, beaten
60ml/4 tbsp cooked rice or stale breadcrumbs
salt and ground black pepper

For the sauce
45ml/3 tbsp plain (all-purpose) flour
350ml/12fl oz/1½ cups turkey giblet stock, warmed
350ml/12fl oz/1½ cups red grape juice
30ml/2 tbsp anis spirit, such as Ricard
salt and ground black pepper

**1** Make the stuffing. Heat 30ml/2 tbsp oil in a pan and fry the onion, garlic and bacon. Remove to a large bowl. Fry the morcilla or black pudding for 3–4 minutes and the liver for 2–3 minutes.

**COOK'S TIP**
Allow 30 minutes to prepare and stuff the bird, and put the turkey in the oven 2¾ hours before carving.

**2** Add the soaked raisins, prunes, almonds, thyme, lemon rind, nutmeg, seasoning and parsley. Stir in the egg and rice or breadcrumbs.

**3** About 3 hours before carving, preheat the oven, with a low shelf, to 200°C/400°F/Gas 6. Remove the turkey's wishbone, running fingernails up the two sides of the neck to find it. Just nick it out. Season the turkey inside, stuff and retruss it. Season outside. Keep at room temperature.

**4** Heat a roasting pan in the oven with 60ml/4 tbsp oil. Put in the turkey and baste the outside. Lay the bacon over the breast and legs. Reduce the oven temperature to 180°C/350°F/Gas 4 and roast for 2¼–2½ hours, basting once. To test, insert a skewer into the thickest part of the inside leg. The juices should run clear. Remove the trussing thread and transfer the turkey to a heated serving plate. Keep warm.

**5** Make the sauce. Skim as much fat as possible from the roasting pan. Sprinkle in the flour and cook gently for a few minutes, stirring. Stir in the warm turkey stock and bring to simmering point. Add the grape juice and anis, and bring back to simmering. Taste for seasoning. Pour into a jug (pitcher). Carve the turkey and serve with the sauce.

**VARIATION**
To make a red stuffing, use frying chorizo instead of morcilla or black pudding. Flavour the stuffing with half a chopped dried chilli, and replace the prunes with chopped green or black olives.

# SPICED DUCK WITH PEARS

*THIS CATALAN SPECIALITY, KNOWN AS ÀNEC AMB PERES IN THE LOCAL LANGUAGE, IS A FABULOUS COMBINATION OF POULTRY AND FRUIT. DUCKS ARE NOT COMMON IN OTHER REGIONS OF SPAIN. TRY TO BUY A BARBARY DUCK IF YOU CAN. THIS DISH FEATURES THE PICADA, A GREAT CATALAN INVENTION MADE OF POUNDED NUTS, WHICH BOTH FLAVOURS AND THICKENS THE FINAL SAUCE. SERVE WITH A BOTTLE OF GRAN SANGRE DE TORO, WHICH WILL STAND UP WELL TO THIS ROBUSTLY FLAVOURED DISH.*

## SERVES SIX

### INGREDIENTS

6 duck portions, preferably Barbary, either breast or leg pieces
15ml/1 tbsp olive oil
1 large onion, thinly sliced
1 cinnamon stick, halved
4 thyme sprigs
475ml/16fl oz/2 cups duck or chicken stock
3 firm, ripe pears
30ml/2 tbsp olive oil
25g/1oz/¼ cup raisins
salt and ground black pepper
young thyme sprigs or fresh parsley, to garnish
mashed potatoes and green vegetables, to serve (optional)

For the picada
30ml/2 tbsp olive oil
½ slice stale bread, without crusts
2 garlic cloves, sliced
15g/½oz/12 almonds, toasted
15g/½oz/12 hazelnuts, toasted
15ml/1 tbsp chopped fresh parsley
salt and ground black pepper

**1** Preheat the oven to 180°C/350°F/ Gas 4. Season the duck portions, pricking the skins with a fork. Fry them, skin side down, for about 5 minutes, until they give off fat. Turn them over and fry on the other side more briefly.

**2** Transfer the duck to an ovenproof dish and drain off all but 15ml/1 tbsp of the fat left in the pan.

**3** Add the onion to the pan and fry for 5 minutes. Add the cinnamon, thyme and stock and bring to the boil. Pour over the duck, reserving a little of the stock, and bake for 1¼ hours.

**4** Make the picada. Heat the olive oil in a frying pan and fry the bread over a high heat. Drain on kitchen paper and reserve. Briefly fry the garlic and reserve with the bread.

**5** Put all the nuts in a mortar and pound, or reduce to a paste in a food processor or blender. Add the bread, torn into pieces, and the garlic, and reduce to a thick, smooth paste with a little pan stock. Add the parsley and seasoning.

**COOK'S TIP**
A good stock is essential for this dish. Buy a large duck (plus two extra duck breasts if you want the portions to be generous) and joint it yourself, using the giblets and carcass for stock. Alternatively, buy duck portions and a carton of chicken stock.

**6** Peel, core and halve the pears. Fry quickly in the oil in the frying pan until beginning to colour on the cut sides.

**7** Add the picada to the ovenproof dish with the raisins and pears. Bake for a further 15 minutes until the pears are tender. Season to taste and garnish with thyme or parsley. Serve with mashed potatoes and vegetables, if you wish.

# BRAISED QUAIL WITH WINTER VEGETABLES

*QUAIL ARE BOTH PLENTIFUL AND VERY POPULAR IN SPAIN, ESPECIALLY DURING THE HUNTING SEASON, WHEN EVERY MAN TURNS OUT WITH A GUN, A DOG AND A KNAPSACK. ROASTING AND BRAISING ARE THE TWO CLASSIC TECHNIQUES FOR COOKING QUAIL. HERE, IN CORDONICES ESTOFADAS, THEY ARE COOKED AND SERVED IN A RED WINE SAUCE, THEN ELEGANTLY DISPLAYED ON CRISP CROÛTES.*

**4** Add more olive oil to the casserole with all the vegetables and shallots. Cook until just colouring. Return the quail to the casserole, breast-sides down, and pour in the red wine. Cover the casserole and transfer to the oven. Cook for about 30 minutes, or until the quail are tender.

**5** Meanwhile, make the croûtes. Using a 10cm/4in plain cutter stamp out rounds from the bread. Heat the oil in a frying pan and cook the bread over a high heat until golden on both sides. Drain on kitchen paper and keep warm.

**6** Place the croûtes on heated plates and set a quail on top of each one. Arrange the vegetables around the quail, cover and keep hot.

**7** Boil the cooking juices hard until reduced to a syrupy consistency. Add the brandy and warm through, then season the sauce with salt and black pepper to taste. Drizzle the sauce over the quail and garnish with parsley, then serve immediately.

SERVES FOUR

INGREDIENTS
    4 quail, cleaned
    175g/6oz small carrots, scrubbed
    175g/6oz baby turnips
    60ml/4 tbsp olive oil
    4 shallots, halved
    450ml/¾ pint/scant 2 cups red wine
    30ml/2 tbsp Spanish brandy
    salt and ground black pepper
    fresh flat leaf parsley, to garnish
For the croûtes
    4 slices stale bread, crusts removed
    60ml/4 tbsp olive oil

**1** Preheat the oven to 220°C/425°F/Gas 7. Season the quail with salt and freshly ground black pepper.

**2** Using a sharp knife, cut the carrots and baby turnips into chunks. (If the carrots are very small, you can leave them whole if you prefer.)

**3** Heat half the olive oil in a flameproof casserole and add the quail. Fry until browned all over, using two wooden spoons or a pair of tongs to turn the birds. Remove from the casserole and set aside.

# MARINATED PIGEON IN RED WINE

*GREAT CLOUDS OF MIGRATING PIGEONS FLY OVER THE MOUNTAINS OF SPAIN TWICE A YEAR, AND SHOOTING THEM IS A BIG SPORT. HERE THEY ARE MARINATED IN SPICED VINEGAR AND RED WINE, THEN COOKED IN THE MARINADE. REARED SQUAB CAN ALSO BE USED. CABBAGE IS A FAMILIAR PARTNER TO PIGEON, BUT PURÉED CELERIAC ALSO GOES VERY WELL.*

SERVES FOUR

INGREDIENTS
   4 pigeons (squabs), each weighing
      about 225g/8oz, cleaned
   30ml/2 tbsp olive oil
   1 onion, roughly chopped
   225g/8oz/3 cups brown cap (cremini)
      mushrooms, sliced
   plain (all-purpose) flour, for dusting
   300ml/½ pint/1¼ cups beef or
      game stock
   30ml/2 tbsp chopped fresh parsley
   salt and ground black pepper
   fresh flat leaf parsley, to garnish
For the marinade
   15ml/1 tbsp olive oil
   1 onion, chopped
   1 carrot, chopped
   1 celery stick, chopped
   3 garlic cloves, sliced
   6 allspice berries, bruised
   2 bay leaves
   8 black peppercorns, bruised
   120ml/4fl oz/½ cup red wine vinegar
   150ml/¼ pint/⅔ cup red wine

**2** Preheat the oven to 150°C/300°F/ Gas 2. Heat the oil in a large, flameproof casserole and cook the onion and mushrooms for about 5 minutes, until the onion has softened.

**3** Meanwhile, remove the pigeons to a plate with a slotted spoon and strain the marinade into a bowl, then set both aside separately.

**4** Sprinkle the flour on the pigeons and add them to the casserole, breast-sides down. Pour in the marinade and stock, and add the chopped parsley and seasoning. Cover and cook for 1½ hours or until tender.

**5** Check the seasoning, then serve the pigeons on warmed plates with the sauce. Garnish with parsley.

**1** Starting a day ahead, combine all the ingredients for the marinade in a large dish. Add the pigeons and turn them in the marinade, then cover and chill for 12 hours, turning occasionally.

**VARIATION**
If you are unable to buy pigeon, this recipe works equally well with rabbit or hare. Buy portions and make deep slashes in the flesh so that the marinade soaks in and flavours right to the centre.

# GUINEA FOWL WITH SAFFRON AND NUT SAUCE

*THE ARABS INTRODUCED SAFFRON TO SPAIN AND THIS IS A MOORISH SAUCE, OF SAFFRON, TOASTED ALMONDS GROUND WITH PARSLEY AND SEVERAL SPICES. PEPITA IS THE SPANISH WORD FOR A SEED OR NUT, HENCE THE NAME PINTADA EN PEPITORIA. SERVE WITH A RIOJA RESERVA, TO DRINK.*

**3** Cut the bird into eight serving pieces, discarding the wing tips, backbone, breastbones and leg tips. This will give you two legs (split them at the joint), two wings with one-third of the breast attached, and two short breast pieces.

**4** Heat the olive oil in a wide shallow flameproof casserole and fry the bread slice on both sides. Fry the garlic quickly, then remove both to a blender.

**5** Season the poultry well and fry them, turning until golden on all sides. Add the remaining stock and the sherry to the pan, stirring to deglaze the pan. Add the bay leaf and thyme and cover. Cook gently for 10 minutes.

**6** Grind together the bread, garlic and almonds. Add the parsley, saffron liquid, nutmeg and cloves, and purée. Stir into the poultry juices, add the lemon juice and paprika, season and serve.

SERVES FOUR

INGREDIENTS
  25g/1oz/¼ cup blanched almonds
  pinch of saffron threads (0.1g)
  120ml/8 tbsp chicken stock
  1.2–1.3kg/2½–3lb guinea fowl
  60ml/4fl oz/½ cup olive oil
  1 thick slice of bread, without crusts
  2 garlic cloves, finely chopped
  120ml/4fl oz/½ cup fino sherry
  1 bay leaf, crumbled
  4 thyme sprigs
  15ml/1 tbsp finely chopped
    fresh parsley
  pinch of freshly grated nutmeg
  pinch of ground cloves
  juice of ½ lemon
  5ml/1 tsp paprika
  salt and ground black pepper

**1** Preheat the oven to 150°C/300°F/Gas 2. Spread the almonds on a baking sheet and toast in the oven for about 20 minutes until golden brown.

**2** Crumble the saffron with your fingers into a jug (pitcher) or small bowl, pour over 30ml/2 tbsp hot chicken stock and leave to soak.

# PERDICES <u>CON</u> UVAS

*PARTRIDGES ARE SPAIN'S COMMONEST GAME BIRDS. THEY HAVE A NATURAL AFFINITY WITH GRAPES,*
*AS WILD BIRDS OFTEN ATTACK THE HARVEST. GAME HENS OR ANY PLUMP SMALL BIRD CAN BE USED*
*FOR THIS POT ROAST, WHERE GRAPES ARE USED FOR THE GARNISH AND THE SAUCE.*

SERVES FOUR

INGREDIENTS
   4 partridges, cleaned
   500g/1¼lb red grapes, split and
      seeded, plus extra to garnish
   45–60ml/3–4 tbsp olive oil
   4 rashers (slices) smoked streaky
      (fatty) bacon, halved across
   1 onion, chopped
   2 garlic cloves, finely chopped
   1 bay leaf
   120ml/4fl oz/½ cup dry white wine
   250ml/8fl oz/1 cup game or
      chicken stock
   freshly grated nutmeg
   salt and ground black pepper
   30ml/2 tbsp chopped fresh parsley,
      to garnish

**2** Fry the bacon until crisp, then reserve on a plate. Put the birds into the casserole breast sides down and fry until coloured. Turn them with two spoons, frying and turning until brown all over. Remove.

**3** Fry the onion and garlic, adding a little more oil if needed, until softened.

**4** Return the birds to the casserole and arrange two pieces of bacon on top of each. Push 125g/5oz grapes in round them, and add the bay leaf. Pour in the white wine and stock. Add plenty of black pepper. Simmer, covered, for 30 minutes.

**5** Remove the birds and bacon to a plate. Spoon the casserole contents into a food processor, discarding the bay leaf, and purée. Add plenty of nutmeg and check the seasoning.

**6** Return the birds to the pan, pour the sauce around them, and add 125g/5oz grapes. Heat through. Serve, garnished with extra grapes, crumbled bacon and a little parsley.

**1** Season the birds inside and out, then stuff with 250g/9oz grapes. Put 45ml/ 3 tbsp oil in a flameproof casserole into which the birds will fit snugly.

# MEAT AND GAME

*From Liver and Bacon Casserole to Rabbit Salmorejo
and the ever-popular beef with a blue cheese sauce,
there are dishes for every occasion. Try Stuffed Roast
Loin of Pork, a spring stew of veal with young
vegetables, a lamb dish with Roija, or classic pulse
dishes such as Fabada and Cocido.*

# ALICANTE CRUSTED RICE

*PAELLA CON COSTRA IS AN UNUSUAL PAELLA WITH AN EGG CRUST THAT IS FINISHED IN THE OVEN.*
*THE CRUST SEALS IN ALL THE AROMAS UNTIL IT IS BROKEN OPEN AT THE TABLE.*

SERVES SIX

INGREDIENTS

45ml/3 tbsp olive oil
200g/7oz butifarra, fresh sausages
  or frying chorizo, sliced
2 tomatoes, peeled, seeded
  and chopped
175g/6oz lean cubed pork
175g/6oz skinless, boneless chicken
  breast or rabbit, cut into chunks
350g/12oz/1¾ cups paella rice
900ml–1 litre/1½–1¾ pints/
  3¾–4 cups hot chicken stock
pinch of saffron threads (0.2g)
150g/5oz/⅔ cup cooked chickpeas
6 large (US extra large) eggs
salt and ground black pepper

1 Preheat the oven to 190°C/375°F/
Gas 5. Heat the oil in a flameproof
casserole and fry the sausage until
browned. Add the tomatoes and fry until
reduced. Stir in the pork and chicken or
rabbit pieces and cook for 2–3 minutes
until the meat has browned lightly, stirring.

2 Add the rice to the pan, stir over the
heat for about 1 minute, then pour in
the hot stock. Add the saffron, season
to taste, and stir well.

3 Bring to the boil, then lower the heat
and add the chickpeas. Cover the
casserole tightly with the lid and cook
over a low heat for about 20 minutes or
until the rice is tender.

4 Beat the eggs with a little water and a
pinch of salt and pour over the rice.
Place the casserole, uncovered, in the
oven and cook for about 10 minutes,
until the eggs have set and browned
slightly on top. Serve the paella straight
from the casserole.

# SAN ESTEBAN CANELONES

*CATALANS ARE FOND OF PASTA, AND CANELONES ARE TRADITIONAL ON SAN ESTEBAN, THE DAY AFTER CHRISTMAS DAY, AND ARE OFTEN MADE IN LARGE QUANTITIES. TRY TO KEEP ALL THE CHOPPED STUFFING INGREDIENTS THE SAME SIZE — SMALL DICE. SPANISH STORES SELL SQUARES OF PASTA FOR COOKING THEN ROLLING, BUT READY PREPARED CANNELLONI TUBES HAVE BEEN USED HERE.*

SERVES FOUR TO EIGHT

INGREDIENTS
  60ml/4 tbsp olive oil
  1 onion, finely chopped
  1 carrot, finely chopped
  2 garlic cloves, finely chopped
  2 ripe tomatoes, peeled and
    finely chopped
  2.5ml/½ tsp dried thyme
  150g/5oz raw chicken livers
    or cooked stuffing
  150g/5oz raw pork or cooked ham,
    gammon or sausage
  250g/9oz raw or cooked chicken
  25g/1oz/2 tbsp butter
  5ml/1 tsp fresh thyme
  30ml/2 tbsp brandy
  90ml/6 tbsp crème fraîche or
    double (heavy) cream
  16 no pre-cook cannelloni tubes
  75g/3oz/1 cup grated fresh
    Parmesan cheese
  salt and ground black pepper
  green salad, to serve
For the white sauce
  50g/2oz/¼ cup butter
  50g/2oz/½ cup plain
    (all-purpose) flour
  900ml/1½ pints/3¾ cups milk
  fresh nutmeg, to taste

**1** Heat the oil in a large frying pan, add the onion, carrot, garlic and tomatoes and cook over a low heat, stirring, for about 10 minutes or until very soft. Meanwhile, chop all the meats to the same size, keeping the fresh and cooked meat apart.

**2** Add the butter, then the raw meat, to the centre of the frying pan and cook until coloured. Then add the remaining meats and sprinkle first with thyme, then with the brandy. Stir, then warm through and reduce the liquid.

**3** Pour in the crème fraîche or cream, season to taste and leave to simmer for about 10 minutes. Allow to cool briefly.

**4** Preheat the oven to 190°C/375°F/ Gas 5. Make the white sauce. Melt the butter in a small pan, add the flour and cook, stirring, for 1–2 minutes. Gradually stir in the milk, a little at a time. Bring to simmering point, stirring until the sauce is smooth. Grate in nutmeg to taste, then season with plenty of salt and black pepper.

**5** Spoon a little of the white sauce into a baking dish. Fill the cannelloni tubes with the meat mixture and arrange in a single layer in the dish. Pour the remaining white sauce over them, then sprinkle with the Parmesan cheese. Bake for 35–40 minutes, or until the pasta is tender. Leave for 10 minutes before serving with green salad.

# FABADA

*THIS BEAN AND SAUSAGE HOTPOT FROM THE WILD MOUNTAINS OF ASTURIAS ON THE NORTHERN COAST OF SPAIN, HAS ACHIEVED WORLD FAME. IT USED TO CONTAIN DRIED BROAD (FAVA) BEANS, WHICH GAVE IT THE NAME, BUT WHEN THESE OLD-FASHIONED BEANS WERE ABANDONED AND MODERN FABES — WHITE KIDNEY BEANS — WERE ADOPTED, IT BECAME A TRULY GREAT DISH. CURED SAUSAGES, A PORK KNUCKLE AND BELLY PORK LEND THE BEANS AN INCREDIBLE RICHNESS, WHICH IS ENHANCED BY SAFFRON AND PAPRIKA. IT IS A GOOD DISH FOR WINTER EVENINGS, SERVED WITH GLASSES OF CIDER.*

SERVES EIGHT

INGREDIENTS

  500–800g/1¼–1¾ lb belly pork,
    in thick slices
  1 smoked gammon (smoked or cured
    ham) knuckle, about 675g/1½ lb,
    skin slashed
  800g/1¾ lb dried cannellini beans,
    soaked overnight (see Cook's Tip)
  5ml/1 tsp black peppercorns, crushed
  15ml/1 tbsp paprika
  pinch of saffron threads (0.2g)
  1 bay leaf
  30ml/2 tbsp oil (optional)
  4 garlic cloves, chopped
  3 red chorizo sausages, thickly sliced
  175g/6oz *morcilla* or black
    pudding (blood sausage),
    thickly sliced
  ground black pepper (optional)

**1** Using a very large stockpot (with a capacity of at least 6 litres/10 pints/ 25 cups), put the pork belly and knuckle into the pot with water to cover. Bring to the boil, then drain the meat and return it to the stockpot.

**COOK'S TIP**
The quality of the bean is a feature of the dish so try to use luxury Spanish beans, now widely exported. Fabes are like very large, white cannellini beans. If luxury Spanish beans are unavailable use lingots (the French *cassoulet* bean) or large white kidney bean.

**2** Add the drained beans to the pot and pour over 2.3 litres/4 pints/10 cups water. Bring to the boil very slowly, then boil for 10 minutes. Reduce the heat and add the peppercorns, paprika, crumbled saffron and the bay leaf.

**3** Simmer very gently over a very low heat for 2 hours. (It is best to put the pot over a small burner, turned low.) Check occasionally that the beans are still covered with liquid, but do not stir energetically or the beans will break up.

**4** Remove the pork belly and knuckle and set them aside to cool. Strip off the skin and fat, and take 30ml/2 tbsp chopped fat for frying (or use oil). Heat this in a frying pan and cook the garlic lightly, then spoon it into the beans.

**VARIATION**
Most Spanish bean stews are flavoured with meat from the pig and are then enriched with pork fat. However, in the north, beans are cooked with clams.

**5** Fry the chorizo and morcilla or black pudding lightly in the same pan. Gently stir into the bean pot.

**6** Remove all the meat from the ham bone. Chop it with the pork and return to the stockpot. Simmer for a few minutes. Check the seasonings (there should be enough salt from the meat already) and serve.

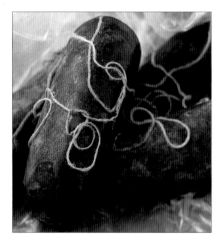

# LIVER AND BACON CASSEROLE

*IN SPAIN, LIVER MEANS PIG'S LIVER, AND IS COOKED HERE IN A WELL-SEASONED SAUCE. LAMBS ARE KILLED WHEN THEY ARE VERY SMALL AND THE LIVER IS NOT MUCH OF A MEAL. THE PIG'S LIVER IS THE FIRST THING TO BE EATEN FROM THE NEW PIG, AND SO IS ASSOCIATED WITH ONE OF THE BIG FEASTS OF THE YEAR, MATANZA. YOU CAN SUBSTITUTE LAMB'S LIVER IF YOU PREFER.*

SERVES THREE TO FOUR

INGREDIENTS
  450g/1lb pig's or lamb's liver,
    trimmed and sliced
  60ml/4 tbsp milk (for pig's liver)
  30ml/2 tbsp olive oil
  225g/8oz rindless smoked lean bacon
    rashers (strips), cut into pieces
  2 onions, halved and sliced
  175g/6oz/2¼ cups brown cap
    (cremini) mushrooms, halved
  25g/1oz/2 tbsp butter
  30ml/2 tbsp plain (all-purpose) flour
  150ml/¼ pint/⅔ cup hot
    chicken stock
  15ml/1 tbsp soy sauce
  5ml/1 tsp paprika
  salt and ground black pepper

**1** If using pig's liver, soak it in the milk for 1 hour for a milder flavour, then blot dry with kitchen paper.

**2** Heat the oil in a frying pan and stir-fry the bacon until crisp. Add the onion and cook, stirring, until softened. Add the mushrooms and fry for 1 minute.

**3** Using a slotted spoon, remove the bacon and vegetables from the pan and keep warm. Add the liver to the fat remaining in the pan and cook over a high heat for 3–4 minutes, turning once to seal the slices on both sides. Remove from the pan and keep warm.

**4** Melt the butter in the pan, sprinkle the flour over and cook briefly. Stir in the stock, soy sauce and paprika and bring to a simmer. Return the liver and vegetables. Simmer gently for 3–4 minutes. Check the seasoning.

**VARIATION**
Bread is the classic accompaniment to this dish, but macaroni or a choice of vegetables make equally good partners.

# STUFFED ROAST LOIN OF PORK

*PORK IS SPAIN'S MOST POPULAR MEAT, THE LOIN PARTICULARLY SO. FOR THIS DISH, LOMO DE CERDO RELLENO, YOU NEED THE WHOLE CUT WITH THE FLAP ON THE SIDE TO ENCLOSE THE STUFFING, WHICH IS RICHLY FLAVOURED WITH FIGS. MEAT AND FRUIT ARE A POPULAR CATALAN COMBINATION.*

SERVES FOUR

INGREDIENTS

60ml/4 tbsp olive oil
1 onion, finely chopped
2 garlic cloves, chopped
75g/3oz/1½ cups stale breadcrumbs
4 ready-to-eat dried figs, chopped
8 pitted green olives, chopped
25g/1oz/¼ cup flaked almonds
15ml/1 tbsp lemon juice
15ml/1 tbsp chopped fresh parsley
1 egg yolk
1kg/2¼lb boned loin of pork with
the side flap attached
salt, paprika and black pepper

**1** Preheat the oven to 200°C/400°F/ Gas 6. Heat 45ml/3 tbsp of the oil in a pan, add the onion and garlic, and cook gently until softened. Remove the pan from the heat, and stir in the breadcrumbs, figs, olives, almonds, lemon juice, parsley and egg yolk. Season with salt, paprika and pepper.

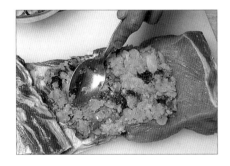

**2** Remove any string from the pork and unroll the belly flap, cutting away any excess fat or meat to enable you to do so. Spread half the stuffing over the flat piece and roll it up, starting from the thick side. Tie the joint at intervals with string to hold it together.

**3** Pour the remaining oil into a small roasting pan and add the pork. Roast for 1¼ hours. Meanwhile, form the remaining stuffing mixture into balls and add to the pan, 15–20 minutes before the end of cooking time.

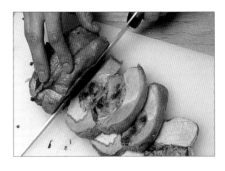

**4** Remove the pork from the oven and leave it rest for 10 minutes. Carve into thick slices and serve with the stuffing balls and any juices from the pan. This dish is also good served cold.

# SKEWERED LAMB WITH RED ONION SALSA

*THE MOORS FIRST INTRODUCED SKEWERED AND BARBECUED MEAT TO SPAIN, WHERE IT HAS BEEN POPULAR FOR OVER 1,500 YEARS. THESE SPICED SKEWERS ARE ACCOMPANIED BY A SIMPLE SALSA.*

SERVES FOUR

INGREDIENTS
  500–675g/1¼–1½lb ready-trimmed,
    cubed lamb
  5ml/1 tsp ground cumin
  10ml/2 tsp paprika
  30ml/2 tbsp olive oil
  salt and ground black pepper
For the red onion salsa
  1 red onion, very thinly sliced
  1 large tomato, seeded
    and chopped
  15ml/1 tbsp red wine vinegar
  3–4 fresh basil or mint leaves,
    roughly torn

**VARIATION**
Skewer squares of (bell) pepper, and whole bay leaves between the cubes of spicy, marinated meat.

**1** Season the lamb with the cumin, paprika, oil and black pepper. Toss well to coat. Leave in a cool place for several hours, or in the refrigerator overnight, so that the lamb absorbs all the spicy flavours.

**2** Spear the cubes of lamb on four skewers, leaving one end of each of the skewers free for picking up.

**3** To make the salsa, put the sliced onion, tomato, vinegar and basil or mint leaves in a small bowl and stir together. Season to taste with salt and pepper.

**4** If cooking on a barbecue, the charcoal should be grey with no flames before you start cooking. Alternatively, preheat the grill (broiler) with the shelf about 15cm/6in from the heat source. Generously brush the grill pan with oil.

**5** Season the lamb with salt and cook for 5–10 minutes, turning the skewers occasionally, until the lamb is well browned but still slightly pink in the centre. Serve hot, with the salsa.

**COOK'S TIP**
If using wooden skewers, soak them in cold water first, to prevent them burning.

# COCHIFRITO

*ARAGON AND NAVARRE IN THE PYRENEES ARE KNOWN FOR THEIR FINE INGREDIENTS — AND ALSO FOR THEIR SIMPLE COOKING. "IF THE QUALITY IS THERE, NO NEED TO EMPLOY TRICKS IN THE KITCHEN" RUNS THE SPANISH PROVERB. THE MEAT IS FRIED SIMPLY AND FLAVOURED WITH LEMON JUICE AND PAPRIKA IN THIS DISH. IT CAPTURES THE VERY ESSENCE OF LAMB.*

SERVES FOUR

INGREDIENTS
  800g/1¾lb very well-trimmed,
    tender lamb (see Cook's Tip),
    in cubes or strips
  30ml/2 tbsp olive oil, plus extra
  1 onion, chopped
  2 garlic cloves, finely chopped
  5ml/1 tsp paprika
  juice of 2 lemons
  15ml/1 tbsp finely chopped
    fresh parsley
  salt and ground black pepper

**COOK'S TIP**
The sweetest lamb is cut from the shoulder. However, it also contains quite a lot of fat, often in layers through the meat, so allow extra weight, and cut it out.

**1** Season the lamb with salt and ground black pepper. Heat the 30ml/2 tbsp olive oil in a large frying pan or casserole over a high heat and add the meat in handfuls. Add the onion at the same time, and keep pushing the meat around the pan with a spatula. Add more meat to the pan as each batch is sealed. Add the chopped garlic and a little more oil if necessary.

**2** When the meat is golden and the onion soft, sprinkle with paprika and lemon juice. Cover and simmer for 15 minutes. Check the seasonings and add a dusting of parsley, then serve.

**VARIATION**
This dish may also be made using pork in place of the lamb – the name cochifrito means little pig, fried.

# LAMB WITH RED PEPPERS AND RIOJA

*WORLD-FAMOUS FOR ITS RED WINE, RIOJA ALSO PRODUCES EXCELLENT RED PEPPERS. IT EVEN HAS A RED PEPPER FAIR, AT LODOSO, EVERY YEAR. TOGETHER THEY GIVE THIS LAMB STEW A LOVELY RICH FLAVOUR. BOILED POTATOES MAKE A VERY GOOD ACCOMPANIMENT.*

SERVES FOUR

INGREDIENTS
  15ml/1 tbsp plain (all-purpose) flour
  1kg/2¼lb lean lamb, cubed
  60ml/4 tbsp olive oil
  2 red onions, sliced
  4 garlic cloves, sliced
  10ml/2 tsp paprika
  1.5ml/¼ tsp ground cloves
  400ml/14fl oz/1⅔ cups red Rioja
  150ml/¼ pint/⅔ cup lamb stock
  2 bay leaves
  2 thyme sprigs
  3 red (bell) peppers, halved
    and seeded
  salt and ground black pepper
  bay leaves and thyme sprigs,
    to garnish (optional)

1 Preheat the oven to 160°C/325°F/ Gas 3. Season the flour, add the lamb and toss lightly to coat.

2 Heat the oil in a frying pan and fry the lamb until browned. Transfer to an ovenproof dish. Fry the onions and garlic until soft. Add to the meat.

3 Add the paprika, cloves, Rioja, lamb stock, bay leaves and thyme and bring the mixture to a gentle simmer. Add the halved red peppers. Cover the dish with a lid or foil and cook for about 30 minutes, or until the meat is tender. Garnish with more bay leaves and thyme sprigs, if you like.

# VEAL CASSEROLE WITH BROAD BEANS

*THIS DELICATE STEW, FLAVOURED WITH SHERRY AND PLENTY OF GARLIC, IS A SPRING DISH MADE WITH NEW VEGETABLES — MENESTRA DE TERNERA. FOR A DELICIOUS FLAVOUR BE SURE TO ADD PLENTY OF PARSLEY JUST BEFORE SERVING. LAMB IS EQUALLY GOOD COOKED IN THIS WAY.*

### SERVES SIX

INGREDIENTS

  45ml/3 tbsp olive oil
  1.3–1.6kg/3–3½lb veal, cut into
    5cm/2in cubes
  1 large onion, chopped
  6 large garlic cloves, unpeeled
  1 bay leaf
  5ml/1 tsp paprika
  240ml/8fl oz/1 cup fino sherry
  100g/4oz/scant 1 cup shelled,
    skinned broad (fava) beans
  60ml/4 tbsp chopped fresh flat
    leaf parsley
salt and ground black pepper

**1** Heat 30ml/2 tbsp oil in a large flameproof casserole. Add half the meat and brown well on all sides. Transfer to a plate. Brown the rest of the meat and remove from the pan.

**2** Add the remaining oil to the pan and cook the onion until soft. Return the meat to the casserole and stir well to mix with the onion.

**3** Add the garlic cloves, bay leaf, paprika and sherry. Season with salt and black pepper. Bring to simmering point, then cover and cook very gently for 30–40 minutes.

**4** Add the broad beans to the casserole about 10 minutes before the end of the cooking time. Check the seasoning and stir in the chopped parsley just before serving.

# COCIDO

*THE SPANISH NATIONAL DISH, COCIDO IS ALSO MADRID'S MOST FAMOUS STEW. THE NAME SIMPLY MEANS "BOILED DINNER" AND IT USED TO BE MADE MORE THAN ONCE A WEEK. A POT OF FRESH AND SALT MEAT WITH CHICKEN AND SAUSAGES IS SIMMERED WITH CHICKPEAS AND SOME FRESH VEGETABLES. THE BROTH MAKES A SOUP COURSE AND THEN THE REST IS DISPLAYED ON TWO SPLENDID PLATTERS. SERVE WITH A BOTTLE OF VIÑA ARANA FROM LA RIOJA ALTA OR BODEGAS BILBAINAS VIÑA POMAL.*

SERVES EIGHT

INGREDIENTS

  500–800g/1¼–1¾lb cured brisket
    or silverside (pot roast)
  250g/9oz smoked streaky (fatty)
    bacon, in one piece, or 250g/9oz
    belly pork
  1 knuckle gammon (smoked or cured
    ham) bone, with some meat
    still attached
  500–750g/1¼–1¾lb beef marrow
    bone, sawn through
  1 pig's trotter (foot), sawn through
  1 whole garlic bulb
  2 bay leaves
  5ml/1 tsp black peppercorns,
    lightly crushed
  250g/9oz/1¼ cups dried chickpeas,
    soaked overnight and drained
  2 quarters corn-fed chicken
  1 small onion, studded with
    2 or 3 cloves
  2 large carrots, cut into big pieces
  2 leeks, cut into chunks
  500g/1¼lb small new potatoes,
    scrubbed
  2 red chorizo sausages
  1 morcilla or 250g/9oz black pudding
    (blood sausage)
  30ml/2 tbsp long grain rice
  1 small (bell) pepper, finely diced
  salt

**1** Put the salt meat – brisket or silverside, bacon or pork and knuckle – into a large pan and cover with water. Bring slowly to the boil, simmer for 5 minutes to remove excess salt, and drain.

**VARIATIONS**
The types of meat used in this hearty stew can be varied. Just make sure that you include a salty meat, a meat on the bone, a smoked meat, a piece of pork, a piece of beef and a piece of chicken – plus a paprika sausage.

**2** Using a very large stockpot (with a capacity of at least 6 litres/10 pints/ 5 quarts), pack in all the meat, skin side down, with the marrowbone and trotter. Add the garlic bulb, bay leaves and peppercorns, with water to cover. Bring to simmering point, skimming off any scum, with a slotted spoon.

**3** Add the drained chickpeas, cover and simmer on the lowest possible heat for 1½ hours, checking occasionally that there is enough liquid.

**4** Add the chicken and onion to the pot. Cook until the chickpeas are done.

**5** Start the vegetables. Put the carrots, leeks and potatoes into a large pan with the chorizo (but not the morcilla or black pudding). Cover with water and bring to the boil. Simmer for 25 minutes, until the potatoes are cooked. About 5 minutes before the end, add the morcilla or black pudding.

**6** Strain off enough broth from the meat pot (about 1.2 litres/2 pints/5 cups) into a pan, for soup. Bring back to the boil, sprinkle in the rice and cook for 15 minutes. Add the diced pepper and cook for 2–3 minutes more. Serve the soup as the first course.

**7** Drain the vegetables and sausages and arrange on a platter. Serve as a separate second course or as an accompaniment with the meat.

**8** Slice the meats, removing the marrow from the bone and adding it to the chickpeas. Arrange with all the meats on a heated serving platter, moistening with a little broth.

# ROPA VIEJA

*THE NAME OF THIS DISH MEANS "OLD CLOTHES", WHICH SOUNDS A GOOD DEAL MORE ROMANTIC THAN LEFTOVERS. IT IS A DISH FOR USING UP MEATS FROM THE COCIDO, AND THE RECIPE SHOWS BOTH JEWISH AND ARAB INFLUENCES. IT IS NORMALLY MADE WITH COLD ROAST BEEF, BUT IT IS IDEAL FOR FINISHING UP COLD TURKEY AND OTHER CHRISTMAS MEATS AND EVEN STUFFING.*

**3** If using the fresh pepper, add it to the casserole and stir-fry until softened.

**4** Add the tomatoes and the chopped baked pepper, if using, the meat stock, cumin, allspice, ground cloves and cayenne pepper. Season to taste. Add the cubed meat and simmer gently.

**5** Heat 45ml/3 tbsp oil over a high heat in a large frying pan. Fry the aubergine cubes, in batches if necessary, until they are brown on all sides. (If you need to add more oil, add it to an empty pan, and reheat to a high heat, before adding more aubergine cubes.)

**6** Add the aubergine and chickpeas to the casserole and bring to a simmer, adding a little more stock to cover, if necessary – the dish should be almost solid. Check the seasonings, garnish with mint, if using, and serve.

SERVES FOUR

INGREDIENTS
  2 small aubergines (eggplant)
  90ml/6 tbsp olive oil
  1 large onion, chopped
  3 garlic cloves, finely chopped
  1 fresh, or baked, red (bell) pepper,
    seeded and sliced (optional)
  400g/14oz can tomatoes
  250ml/8fl oz/1 cup meat stock
  2.5ml/½ tsp ground cumin
  2.5ml/½ tsp ground allspice
  pinch of ground cloves
  2.5ml/½ tsp cayenne pepper
  400g/14oz cooked beef, cubed
    (or mixed turkey, ham, etc)
  400g/14oz can chickpeas, drained
  salt and ground black pepper
  chopped fresh mint, to garnish
    (optional)

**1** Cut the aubergines into cubes and put them into a colander. Sprinkle with 10ml/2 tsp salt, turning the cubes over with your hands. Leave to drain for about 1 hour. Rinse, then squeeze them dry using kitchen paper.

**2** Meanwhile put 30ml/2 tbsp oil in a wide flameproof casserole and fry the onion and garlic until soft.

# SOLOMILLO WITH CABRALES SAUCE

*WELL-HUNG BEEF IS A FEATURE OF THE BASQUE COUNTRY, SERVED HERE WITH CABRALES, THE BLUE CHEESE FROM SPAIN'S NORTHERN MOUNTAINS. FRENCH ROQUEFORT IS ALSO EXTREMELY POPULAR, BECAUSE IT APPEALS TO THE SPANISH LOVE OF SALTY FLAVOURS. IN THIS RECIPE THE SALT AND BRANDY IN THE SAUCE ARE PERFECTLY BALANCED BY THE CREAM.*

SERVES FOUR

INGREDIENTS
   25g/1oz/2 tbsp butter
   30ml/2 tbsp olive oil
   4 fillet steaks, cut 5cm/2in thick,
      about 150g/5oz each
   salt and coarsely ground black pepper
   fresh flat leaf parsley, to garnish
For the blue cheese sauce
   30ml/2 tbsp Spanish brandy
   150ml/5fl oz/⅔ cup double
      (heavy) cream
   75g/3oz *Cabrales* or Roquefort
      cheese, crumbled

**COOK'S TIP**
Cabrales is also known as Picón and Treviso and has a slightly more acidic flavour than Roquefort.

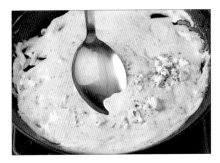

**1** Heat the butter and oil together in a heavy frying pan, over a high heat. Season the steaks well. Fry them for 2 minutes on each side, to sear them.

**2** Lower the heat slightly and cook for a further 2–3 minutes on each side, or according to your taste. Remove the steaks to a warm plate.

**3** Reduce the heat and add the brandy, stirring to pick up the juices. Add the cream and boil to reduce a little.

**4** Add the crumbled cheese and mash it into the sauce using a spoon. Taste for seasoning. Serve in a small sauce jug (pitcher), or poured over the steaks. Garnish the beef with parsley.

# VENISON CHOPS WITH ROMESCO SAUCE

*ROMESCO IS THE CATALAN WORD FOR THE ÑORA CHILLI. IT LENDS A SPICY ROUNDNESS TO ONE OF SPAIN'S GREATEST SAUCES, FROM TARRAGONA. THE SAUCE ALSO CONTAINS GROUND TOASTED NUTS AND OFTEN ANOTHER FIERCER CHILLI. IT CAN BE SERVED COLD, AS A DIP FOR VEGETABLES, BUT THIS SPICY VERSION IS THE IDEAL PARTNER FOR GAME CHOPS — VENADO CON ROMESCO. BOAR CHOPS CAN ALSO BE USED BUT NEED LONGER COOKING. CHOOSE GRAN SANGRE DE TORO TO DRINK.*

**4** Add the soaked chillies and tomatoes to the processor or blender. Tip in the garlic, with the oil from the pan and blend the mixture to form a smooth paste.

**5** With the motor running, gradually add the remaining olive oil and then the sherry and wine vinegars. When the sauce is smooth and well blended, scrape it into a bowl and season with salt and ground black pepper to taste. Cover with clear film (plastic wrap) and chill for 2 hours.

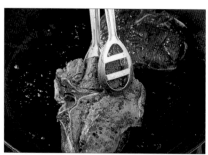

SERVES FOUR

INGREDIENTS
  4 venison chops, cut 2cm/¾in thick
    and about 175–200g/6–7oz each
  30ml/2 tbsp olive oil
  50g/2oz/4 tbsp butter
  braised Savoy cabbage, to serve
For the sauce
  3 ñora chillies
  1 hot dried chilli
  25g/1oz/¼ cup almonds
  150ml/¼ pint/⅔ cup olive oil
  1 slice stale bread, crusts removed
  3 garlic cloves, chopped
  3 tomatoes, peeled, seeded and
    roughly chopped
  60ml/4 tbsp sherry vinegar
  60ml/4 tbsp red wine vinegar
  salt and ground black pepper

**1** To make the romesco sauce, slit the chillies and remove the seeds, then leave the chillies to soak in warm water for about 30 minutes until soft. Drain the chillies, dry them on kitchen paper and chop finely.

**2** Dry-fry the almonds in a frying pan over a medium heat, shaking the pan occasionally, until the nuts are toasted evenly. Transfer the nuts to a food processor or blender.

**3** Add 45ml/3 tbsp oil to the frying pan and fry the bread slice until golden on both sides. Lift it out with a slotted spoon and drain on kitchen paper. Tear the bread and add to the food processor or blender. Fry the chopped garlic in the oil remaining in the pan.

**6** Season the chops with pepper. Heat the olive oil and butter in a heavy frying pan and fry the chops for about 5 minutes each side until golden brown and cooked through.

**7** When the chops are almost cooked, transfer the romesco sauce to a pan and heat it gently. If it is too thick, stir in a little boiling water.

**8** Serve the sauce with the chops, accompanied by braised cabbage.

# RABBIT SALMOREJO

*THE CARTHAGINIANS NAMED SPAIN "RABBIT LAND" AND THE ROMANS KEPT THE NAME, REFERRING TO THE COUNTRY AS HISPANIA. THE MODERN NAME, ESPAÑA, IS CLEARLY DERIVED FROM THIS OLD NAME AND SERVES TO REMIND US HOW COMMON RABBITS ARE THROUGHOUT SPAIN. THIS IS AN UPDATED VERSION OF ONE OF THE CLASSIC MEDITERRANEAN RABBIT STEWS. SALMOREJO INDICATES POUNDED GARLIC, BREAD AND VINEGAR, WHILE WINE IS A MODERN TOUCH.*

### SERVES FOUR

INGREDIENTS

675g/1½lb rabbit, jointed
300ml/½ pint/1¼ cups dry
  white wine
15ml/1 tbsp sherry vinegar
several oregano sprigs
2 bay leaves
30ml/2 tbsp plain (all-purpose) flour
90ml/6 tbsp olive oil
175g/6oz baby (pearl) onions,
  peeled and left whole
4 garlic cloves, sliced
150ml/¼ pint/⅔ cup chicken stock
1 dried chilli, seeded and
  finely chopped
10ml/2 tsp paprika
salt and ground black pepper
fresh flat leaf parsley sprigs,
  to garnish (optional)

**1** Put the rabbit in a bowl. Add the wine, vinegar, oregano and bay leaves and toss together. Marinate for several hours or overnight in the refrigerator.

**2** Drain the rabbit, reserving the marinade, and pat it dry with kitchen paper. Season the flour and use to dust the marinated rabbit.

**3** Heat the oil in a large, wide flameproof casserole or frying pan. Fry the rabbit pieces until golden on all sides, then remove them and set aside. Fry the onions until they are beginning to colour, then reserve on a separate plate.

**4** Add the garlic to the pan and fry, then add the strained marinade, with the chicken stock, chilli and paprika.

**5** Return the rabbit and the reserved onions to the pan. Bring to a simmer, then cover and simmer gently for about 45 minutes until the rabbit is tender. Check the seasoning, adding more vinegar and paprika if necessary. Serve the dish garnished with a few sprigs of flat leaf parsley, if you like.

**COOK'S TIP**
If you wish, rather than cooking on the stove, transfer the stew to an ovenproof dish and bake in the oven at 180°C/350°F/Gas 4 for about 50 minutes.

# DESSERTS

*Iced desserts were introduced to Spain by the Moors,*
*who also created luxurious dishes of fruit in syrup.*
*Caramel is a much-loved flavour and used to sweeten*
*Spanish custard dishes, which can be baked with a*
*caramel syrup or served with a crisp caramel topping.*

# RUM AND RAISIN ICE CREAM

*HELADO CON RON Y PASAS IS AN ICE CREAM WITH A LONG TRADITION IN SPAIN. DARK RUM COMES FROM THE FORMER SPANISH ISLAND OF CUBA, WHILE THE MALAGA REGION PRODUCES SOME OF THE BEST MUSCATEL RAISINS IN THE WORLD, HUGE AND BLACK — THOUGH FROM A WHITE GRAPE.*

SERVES FOUR TO SIX

INGREDIENTS
150g/5oz/1 cup large Muscatel
    raisins, Malagan if possible
60ml/4 tbsp dark rum
4 egg yolks
75g/3oz/6 tbsp light brown sugar
5ml/1 tsp cornflour (cornstarch)
300ml/½ pint/1¼ cups full-fat
    (whole) milk
300ml/½ pint/1¼ cups
    whipping cream
wafers or biscuits (cookies), to serve

**1** Put the raisins in a bowl, add the rum and mix well. Cover and leave to soak for 3–4 hours or overnight.

**2** Whisk together the egg yolks, sugar and cornflour in a large bowl until the mixture is thick and foamy. Heat the milk in a large heavy pan to just below boiling point.

**3** Whisk the milk into the eggs, then pour back into the pan. Cook over a gentle heat, stirring with a wooden spoon, until the custard thickens and is smooth. Leave to cool.

**4** Whip the cream until it is just thick but still falls from a spoon, then fold it into the cold custard. If you have an ice cream maker, pour the mixture into the machine tub, then churn until thick. Transfer to a freezerproof container. Working by hand, pour the mixture into a plastic tub or similar freezerproof container. Freeze for 4 hours, beating once in a food processor after 2 hours, then beat again after 4 hours.

**5** Fold the soaked raisins into the soft ice cream, then cover and freeze for 2–3 hours, or until it is firm enough to scoop. Serve in bowls or tall glasses, with wafers or dessert biscuits.

# SORBETE ᴰᴱ LIMÓN

*THE MOORS INTRODUCED ICES TO ANDALUCIA A THOUSAND YEARS AGO. EATING THIS SMOOTH, TANGY SORBET, YOU CAN IMAGINE YOURSELF IN A PALACE LIKE THE ONE AT GRANADA, LOUNGING ON SILKEN CUSHIONS, WITH THE STARS ABOVE, NIGHTINGALES SINGING AND THE FOUNTAINS TINKLING.*

SERVES SIX

INGREDIENTS
   200g/7oz/1 cup caster
      (superfine) sugar
   300ml/¼l pint/1¼ cups water
   4 lemons, washed
   1 large (US extra large) egg white
   a little granulated sugar,
      for sprinkling

**1** Put the sugar and water into a heavy pan and bring slowly to the boil, stirring occasionally, until the sugar has just dissolved.

**2** Using a swivel vegetable peeler, pare the rind thinly from two of the lemons directly into the pan. Simmer for about 2 minutes without stirring, then remove the pan from the heat. Leave the syrup to cool, then chill.

**3** Squeeze the juice from all the lemons and carefully strain it into the syrup, making sure all the pips are removed. Take the lemon rind out of the syrup and set it aside until you make the garnish.

**4** If you have an ice cream maker, strain the syrup into the machine tub and churn for 10 minutes until thickening.

**5** Lightly whisk the egg white with a fork and pour it into the machine. Continue to churn for 10–15 minutes, until firm enough to scoop.

**6** Working by hand, strain the syrup into a plastic tub or a similar shallow freezerproof container and freeze for 4 hours, until the mixture is mushy.

**7** Scoop the mushy mixture into a food processor and beat until smooth. Lightly whisk the egg white with a fork until it is just frothy. Spoon the sorbet back into its container and beat in the egg white. Return to the freezer for 1 hour.

**8** To make the sugared rind garnish, use the blanched rind from step 2. Cut into very thin strips and sprinkle with granulated sugar on a plate. Scoop the sorbet into bowls or glasses and decorate with sugared lemon rind.

**VARIATION**
Sorbet (sherbet) can be made from any citrus fruit. As a guide, you will need 300ml/½ pint/1¼ cups of fresh fruit juice and the pared rind of half the squeezed fruits. For example, use four oranges or two oranges and two lemons, or, to make a grapefruit sorbet, use the rind of one ruby grapefruit and the juice of two.

# HONEY-BAKED FIGS WITH HAZELNUT ICE CREAM

*TWO WILD INGREDIENTS – FIGS AND HAZELNUTS – ARE USED TO MAKE THIS DELECTABLE DESSERT, HIGOS CON HELADO DE AVELLANA. FRESH FIGS ARE BAKED IN A LIGHTLY SPICED LEMON AND HONEY SYRUP AND ARE SERVED WITH HOME-MADE ROASTED HAZELNUT ICE CREAM.*

### SERVES FOUR

INGREDIENTS
   finely pared rind of 1 lemon
   1 cinnamon stick, roughly broken
   60ml/4 tbsp clear honey
   8 large figs
For the hazelnut ice cream
   450ml/¾ pint/scant 2 cups double
      (heavy) cream
   50g/2oz/¼ cup caster
      (superfine) sugar
   3 large (US extra large) egg yolks
   1.5ml/¼ tsp vanilla essence (extract)
   75g/3oz/¾ cup hazelnuts

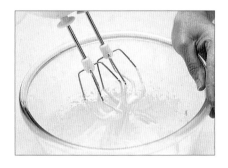

**1** Make the ice cream. Gently heat the cream in a pan until almost boiling. Meanwhile, beat the sugar and egg yolks in a bowl until creamy.

**2** Pour a little hot cream into the egg yolk mixture and stir with a wooden spoon. Pour back into the pan and mix well. Cook over a low heat, stirring constantly, until the mixture thickens slightly and lightly coats the back of the spoon – do not allow it to boil.

**3** Pour the custard into a bowl, stir in the vanilla essence and leave to cool.

**4** Preheat the oven to 180°C/350°F/ Gas 4. Place the hazelnuts on a baking sheet and roast for 10–12 minutes, or until golden. Leave the nuts to cool, then grind them in a food processor.

**5** If you have an ice cream machine, pour in the cold custard and churn until half set. Add the ground hazelnuts and continue to churn until the ice cream is thick. Freeze until firm.

**6** Working by hand, pour the custard into a freezerproof container and freeze for 2 hours, or until the custard feels firm around the edges. Turn into a bowl and beat with an electric whisk or turn into a food processor and beat until smooth. Stir in the hazelnuts and freeze until half set. Beat once more, then freeze until firm.

**7** Preheat the oven to 200°C/400°F/ Gas 6. Remove the ice cream from the freezer and allow to soften slightly.

**8** To make the syrup, put the lemon rind, cinnamon stick, honey and 200ml/ 7fl oz/scant 1 cup water in a small pan and heat slowly until boiling. Simmer the mixture for 5 minutes, then leave to stand for 15 minutes.

**9** Using a sharp knife, cut the figs almost into quarters but leaving the figs still attached at the base. Pack them into a casserole, in a single layer, and pour the honey syrup round and over them. Cover the dish tightly with foil and bake for 10 minutes.

**10** Arrange the figs on small serving plates, with the cooking syrup poured round them. Serve accompanied by a scoop or two of the ice cream.

### COOK'S TIPS
• When toasting the hazelnuts, keep a close eye on them because they can scorch very quickly, spoiling the flavour of the ice cream.
• In southern Spain, red-fleshed figs with a wonderfully sweet flavour grow wild in the scrub.

# BITTER CHOCOLATE MOUSSES

*THE SPANISH INTRODUCED CHOCOLATE TO EUROPE, AND CHOCOLATE MOUSSE REMAINS A FAVOURITE DESSERT IN A COUNTRY THAT USUALLY FAVOURS CUSTARDS AND FRESH FRUIT. THESE DELICIOUS CREMAS DE CHOCOLATE ARE RICH WITH CHOCOLATE, WITH A HINT OF ORANGE LENT BY THE LIQUEUR.*

**2** Whip the cream until soft peaks form, then stir a spoonful into the chocolate mixture to lighten it. Gently fold in the remaining whipped cream.

**3** In a clean, grease-free bowl, use an electric mixer to slowly whisk the egg whites until frothy. Increase the speed and continue until the egg whites form soft peaks. Gradually sprinkle the sugar over the egg whites and continue beating until the whites are stiff and glossy. (Be careful not to over-whisk the eggs.)

**4** Using a rubber spatula or large metal spoon, stir a quarter of the egg whites into the chocolate mixture to lighten it, then gently fold in the remaining whites, cutting down to the bottom of the bowl, along the sides and up to the top in a semicircular motion until they are just combined. Don't worry about a few white streaks.

SERVES EIGHT

INGREDIENTS
  225g/8oz dark (bittersweet)
    chocolate, chopped
  30ml/2 tbsp orange liqueur or a good
    Spanish brandy such as Torres
  50g/2oz/¼ cup unsalted (sweet)
    butter, cut into small pieces
  4 large (US extra large)
    eggs, separated
  90ml/6 tbsp whipping cream
  45ml/3 tbsp caster (superfine) sugar

**COOK'S TIP**
The addition of 1.5ml/¼ tsp cream of tartar to the egg whites helps them to stabilize and hold the volume.

**1** Place the chocolate and 60ml/4 tbsp water in a heavy pan. Melt over a low heat, stirring. Off the heat whisk in the orange liqueur or brandy and butter. Beat the egg yolks until thick and creamy, then slowly beat into the melted chocolate until well blended.

**5** Gently spoon the mixture into eight individual dishes or a 2 litre/3½ pint/ 8 cup bowl. Chill for at least 2 hours until set before serving.

# FLANS

*THESE LITTLE BAKED CARAMEL CUSTARDS, MADE IN BUCKET-SHAPED MOULDS, ARE THE BEST-KNOWN AND MOST POPULAR OF ALL SPANISH DESSERTS. IF YOU DON'T OWN SMALL MOULDS, YOU CAN MAKE ONE LARGE FLAN INSTEAD BUT IT WILL NEED TO BE COOKED FOR A LITTLE LONGER.*

SERVES EIGHT

INGREDIENTS
  250g/9oz/1¼ cups granulated sugar
  1 vanilla pod (bean) or 10ml/2 tsp
    vanilla essence (extract)
  400ml/14fl oz/1⅔ cups milk
  250ml/8fl oz/1 cup whipping cream
  5 large (US extra large) eggs
  2 egg yolks

**1** Select your moulds – eight metal dariole moulds, about 120ml/4fl oz/ ½ cup each, or a soufflé dish 1 litre/ 1¾ pints/4 cups in capacity. Arrange in a roasting pan.

**2** Put 175g/6oz/⅞ cup of the sugar in a small heavy pan with 60ml/4 tbsp water. Bring to the boil over a high heat, swirling the pan to dissolve the sugar. Boil, without stirring, for about 5 minutes until the syrup turns a dark caramel colour.

**3** If using individual moulds, pour a little caramel into each one. If using a single mould, lift it with oven gloves and quickly swirl the dish to coat the base with the caramel. (The caramel will harden quickly as it cools.)

**4** Preheat the oven to 160°C/325°F/ Gas 3. If using, split the vanilla pod lengthways and scrape out the seeds. Pour the milk and cream into a pan, add the vanilla seeds or essence and bring the mixture close to the boil, stirring. Remove from the heat and allow to stand for 15–20 minutes.

**5** In a bowl, whisk the eggs and extra yolks with the remaining sugar for 2–3 minutes until creamy. Whisk in the warm milk and cream mixture, and then strain it into the caramel-lined mould(s). Cover with foil.

**6** Pour boiling water into the pan, to come halfway up the sides of the mould(s). Bake until the custard is just set (20–25 minutes for small moulds; about 40 minutes for a large one. A knife inserted to test should come out clean.) Remove from the water, leave to cool, then chill overnight.

**7** To turn out, run a palette knife around the custard(s). Cover a large mould with a serving dish and, holding tightly, invert the dish and plate together. Lift one edge of the mould, waiting for the caramel to run down, then remove the mould. Cover the small moulds with saucers and invert them to serve.

# CREMA CATALANA

*THIS FABULOUS SPANISH DESSERT OF CREAMY CUSTARD TOPPED WITH A NET OF BRITTLE SUGAR, MAY
WELL BE THE ORIGINAL OF ALL CRÈME BRÛLÉES. CREMAT IS THE CATALAN WORD FOR "BURNT",
AND THIS WAS PROBABLY PART OF ITS ORIGINAL NAME.*

SERVES FOUR

INGREDIENTS
    475ml/16fl oz/2 cups milk
    pared rind of ½ lemon
    1 cinnamon stick
    4 large egg yolks
    105ml/7 tbsp caster
      (superfine) sugar
    25ml/1½ tbsp cornflour (cornstarch)
    ground nutmeg, for sprinkling

**COOK'S TIP**
A special tool known as a quemadora
is sold to caramelize the top of this
dessert. A metal disc on a wooden
handle is heated like a hot poker,
then held over the sugar crust.

**1** Put the milk in a pan with the lemon
rind and cinnamon stick. Bring to the
boil, then simmer for 10 minutes.
Remove the lemon rind and cinnamon.
Put the egg yolks and 45ml/3 tbsp
sugar in a bowl, and whisk until pale
yellow. Add the cornflour and mix well.

**2** Stir a few tablespoons of the hot
milk into the egg yolk mixture, then tip
back into the remaining milk. Return
to the heat and cook gently, stirring, for
about 5 minutes, until thickened and
smooth. Do not boil.

**3** Pour the custard into four shallow
ovenproof dishes, about 13cm/5in in
diameter. Leave to cool, then chill for
a few hours, or overnight, until firm.

**4** No more than 30 minutes before
serving, sprinkle each dessert with
15ml/1 tbsp of the sugar and a little
nutmeg. Preheat the grill (broiler) to
high. Place the dishes under the grill,
on the highest shelf, and cook until the
sugar caramelizes. This will only take
a few seconds and it will caramelize
unevenly. Leave the custards to cool
for a few minutes before serving.

# ARROPE

*THIS IS AN OLD ARAB RECIPE WHOSE NAME MEANS "SYRUP"; THIS VERSION COMES FROM THE PYRENEES REGION. IN SOUTHERN SPAIN, GRAPES, QUINCE AND MELON MIGHT BE USED. ARROPE STARTS AS A LOVELY FRUIT COMPOTE AND ENDS UP AS A SYRUPY JAM, TO BE SCOOPED UP WITH BREAD.*

SERVES TEN

INGREDIENTS
   3 firm peaches, unpeeled
   1kg/2¼ lb/5 cups granulated sugar
   3 large eating apples
   finely grated rind of 1 lemon
   3 firm pears
   finely grated rind of 1 orange
   1 small sweet potato, 150g/5oz
     prepared weight
   200g/7oz butternut squash, peeled
     and prepared weight
   250ml/8fl oz/1 cup dark rum
   30ml/2 tbsp clear honey

**1** Cut the peaches into eighths, without peeling them, and place in the bottom of a large flameproof casserole. Sprinkle with 15ml/1 tbsp of the sugar.

**2** Peel and core the apples and cut them into 16 segments, then arrange on top of the peaches. Sprinkle the lemon rind over the top, along with 15ml/1 tbsp of the sugar. Prepare the pears in the same way as the apples, place in the casserole, then sprinkle over the orange rind, followed by 15ml/1 tbsp of the sugar.

**3** Slice the sweet potato into pieces half the size of the pears and spread them over the top. Prepare the squash in the same way, layering it on top. Sprinkle about 15ml/1 tbsp of the sugar. Cover with a plate that fits inside the rim, and weigh down with a couple of cans. Stand for a minimum of 2 hours (maximum 12) for juice to form.

**4** Remove the cans and plate, put the casserole over a fairly low heat and bring to a simmer. Cook and soften the fruit for 20 minutes, stirring once or twice to prevent sticking.

**5** Add the remaining sugar, in three or four batches, stirring to dissolve each batch before adding the next. Bring the mixture up to a rolling boil, over a medium high heat, and boil very steadily for 45 minutes. Stir and lift off any scum.

**6** The syrup should be considerably reduced. Test by pouring a spoonful on a plate. It should wrinkle when a spoon is pulled across (like jam in the early stages, before a full set is achieved).

**7** Off the heat, add the rum and honey and stir well to combine. Return the casserole to a moderate heat and cook for a further 10 minutes, stirring frequently to prevent the fruit sticking to the base of the pan. The colour will deepen to russet brown. Remove the pan from the heat and set aside to cool.

**8** If the resulting compote is a little too stiff, then stir in some more rum before serving.

**COOK'S TIP**
*Arrope* is immensely rich, so portions should be small. By the time you reach the bottom of the pot it becomes very thick and sticky, and is best scooped up on bits of bread.

# APPLE-STUFFED CRÊPES

*Spain's dairy country lies along the cooler northern coast and crêpes are extremely popular there. The Asturias, which run east to west along the coast, are apple and cider country, too, and crêpes, which are known as* FRISUELOS, *are made with a variety of sweet fillings, such as this succulent apple one.*

**3** Cook the crêpe for about 1 minute until it is golden underneath, then flip it over and cook the other side until golden. Slide the crêpe on to a plate, then repeat with the remaining batter to make seven more. Set the crêpes aside and keep warm.

**4** Make the apple filling. Core the apples and cut them into thick slices. Heat 15g/½oz butter in a large frying pan. Add the apples to the pan and cook until golden on both sides. Transfer the slices to a bowl with a slotted spoon and sprinkle with sugar.

**5** Fold each pancake in half, then fold in half again to form a cone. Fill each with some of the fried apples. Place two filled pancakes on each dessert plate. Drizzle with a little honey and serve at once, accompanied by cream.

SERVES FOUR

INGREDIENTS
   115g/4oz/1 cup plain
    (all-purpose) flour
   pinch of salt
   2 large (US extra large) eggs
   175ml/6fl oz/¾ cup milk
   120ml/4fl oz/½ cup sweet cider
   butter, for frying
   4 eating apples
   60ml/4 tbsp caster (superfine) sugar
   120ml/8 tbsp clear honey, and
    150ml/¼ pint/⅔ cup double (heavy)
    cream, to serve

**COOK'S TIP**
For the best results, use full-fat (whole) milk in the batter.

**1** Make the batter. Sift the flour and salt into a large bowl. Add the eggs and milk and beat until smooth. Stir in the cider. Leave to stand for 30 minutes.

**2** Heat a small heavy non-stick frying pan. Add a little butter and ladle in enough batter to coat the pan thinly.

# HAZELNUT MERINGUES WITH NECTARINES

*MERINGUES GO BACK TO MOORISH TIMES, AND HAZELNUTS, FROM THE WOODED PYRENEES, ARE A POPULAR FLAVOURING. SERVE THEM AS AN ACCOMPANIMENT TO PEACHES IN SYRUP, OR TRY THEM WITH CREAM WHIPPED WITH MALAGA'S DESSERT WINE, AND STUFFED WITH FRESH NECTARINES.*

SERVES FIVE

INGREDIENTS
   3 large (US extra large) egg whites
   175g/6oz/generous ¾ cup caster
      (superfine) sugar
   50g/2oz/½ cup chopped
      hazelnuts, toasted
   300ml/½ pint/1¼ cups double
      (heavy) cream
   60ml/4 tbsp sweet Malaga
      dessert wine
   2 nectarines, stoned (pitted)
      and sliced
   fresh mint sprigs, to decorate

**COOK'S TIP**
Peaches can be used in place of the nectarines, but are better peeled. To remove the skins, place the peaches in a bowl and pour over boiling water to cover. Leave to stand for a few minutes, then drain. The skins should peel off very easily.

**1** Preheat the oven to 140°C/275°F/ Gas 1. Line two large baking sheets with baking parchment.

**2** Whisk the egg whites in a grease-free bowl until they form stiff peaks when the whisks are lifted. Gradually whisk in the caster sugar a spoonful at a time, until a stiff, glossy meringue forms.

**3** Using a large metal spoon, gently fold two-thirds of the chopped toasted hazelnuts into the whisked egg whites.

**4** Divide the meringue mixture between the baking sheets, spooning five ovals on to each one. Scatter the remaining toasted hazelnuts over the meringues on one baking sheet, then flatten the tops of the others using the back of a spoon.

**5** Bake the meringues for 1–1¼ hours until crisp and dry, then lift them off the baking parchment and leave to cool.

**6** Put the cream and dessert wine in a bowl and whisk to form soft peaks. Spoon some of the cream on to each of the plain meringues. Arrange a few nectarine slices on each.

**7** Put one cream-topped meringue and one nut-topped meringue on each dessert plate. Garnish with fresh mint and serve immediately.

# LECHE FRITA <u>WITH</u> BLACK FRUIT SAUCE

*THE NAME OF THIS DESSERT MEANS "FRIED MILK", BUT IT IS REALLY CUSTARD SQUARES. IT IS VERY POPULAR IN THE BASQUE COUNTRY, AND HAS A MELTING, CREAMY CENTRE AND CRUNCHY, GOLDEN COATING. HERE, IT IS SERVED HOT WITH A DARK FRUIT SAUCE, BUT IT IS ALSO GOOD COLD.*

SERVES SIX TO EIGHT

INGREDIENTS
  550ml/18fl oz/2½ cups full-fat
    (whole) milk
  3 finely pared strips of lemon rind
  ½ cinnamon stick
  90g/3½oz/½ cup caster (superfine)
    sugar, plus extra for sprinkling
  60ml/4 tbsp cornflour (cornstarch)
  30ml/2 tbsp plain (all-purpose) flour
  3 large (US extra large) egg yolks
  2 large (US extra large) eggs
  90–120ml/6–8 tbsp stale
    breadcrumbs or dried crumbs
  sunflower oil, for frying
  ground cinnamon, for dusting
For the sauce
  450g/1lb blackcurrants
    or blackberries
  90g/3½oz/½ cup granulated sugar,
    plus extra for dusting

**1** Put the milk, lemon rind, cinnamon stick and sugar in a pan and bring to the boil, stirring gently. Cover and leave to infuse for 20 minutes.

**2** Put the cornflour and flour in a bowl and beat in the egg yolks with a wooden spoon. Add a little of the milk and beat to make a smooth batter.

**3** Strain the remaining hot milk into the batter, then pour back into the pan. Cook over a low heat, stirring constantly. (The mixture won't curdle, but it will thicken unevenly if you let it.) Cook for a couple of minutes, until it thickens and separates from the side of the pan.

**4** Beat the mixture hard with the spoon to ensure a really smooth consistency. Pour into an 18–20cm/7–8in, 1cm/½in-deep rectangular dish, and smooth the top. Cool, then chill until firm.

**5** Make the fruit sauce. Cook the blackcurrants or blackberries with the sugar and a little water for about 10 minutes until soft.

**6** Reserve 30–45ml/2–3 tbsp whole currants or berries, then put the rest in a food processor and blend to make a smooth purée. Return the purée and berries to the pan.

**7** Cut the chilled custard into eight or twelve squares. Beat the eggs in a shallow dish and spread out the breadcrumbs on a plate. Lift half of the squares with a metal spatula into the egg. Coat on both sides, then lift into the crumbs and cover all over. Repeat with the second batch of squares.

**8** Pour about 1cm/½in oil into a deep frying pan and heat until very hot.

**9** Lift two or three coated squares with a palette knife (metal spatula) into the oil and fry for a couple of minutes, shaking or spooning the oil over the top, until golden. Reserve on kitchen paper, while frying the other batches.

**10** To serve, arrange the custard squares on plates and sprinkle with sugar and cinnamon. Pour a circle of warm sauce round the squares, distributing the whole berries evenly.

**COOK'S TIP**
In Spain, milk is usually drunk at breakfast or used for cheese. In northern Spain, the milk has a wonderful quality and has been given special status as a dessert ingredient. Most popular of all the milk desserts are leche frita, flan and filloas (thin pancakes).

# INDEX